ART AND BELIEF

Art and Belief

BY

DAVID W. BOLAM

AND

JAMES L. HENDERSON

SCHOCKEN BOOKS
NEW YORK

Published in U.S.A. in 1969
by Schocken Books Inc.
67 Park Avenue
New York, N.Y. 1001 6
Copyright © 1967 David Bolam & James L. Henderson
Library of Congress Catalog Card
No. 69—12904

Printed in Great Britain

Contents

Illustrations

Acknowledgments

THE authors and publishers would like to thank copyright holders for permission to quote copyright material as follows: On pp. 16 and 84, from *Art and the Creative Unconscious*, by Erich Neumann, transl. by Ralph Mannheim, Bollingen Series LXI (Copyright (c) 1959 by Bollingen Foundation), short quotes from pp. 121 and 118; Alfred A. Knopf for extract on p. 22 from *The Magic Mountain* by Thomas Mann; on p. 23, extract from *Man and his Symbols* by Carl G. Jung, copyright (c) 1964 by Aldus Books Ltd, reprinted by permission of Doubleday & Co. Inc.; The Viking Press Inc. for extract on p. 24 from *Herzog* by Saul Bellow; The Viking Press Inc. for extract on p. 25 from 'Nottingham and the Mining Country' in *Phoenix: The Posthumous Papers of D. H. Lawrence* edited by Edward D. McDonald; 'Encounter' for extracts on pp. 25 and 26 from *A Writer's Notebook* by Albert Camus, transl. by A. Hartley; Harcourt, Brace & World, Inc. for extract on p. 27 from 'The Dry Salvages' from *Four Quartets* by T. S. Eliot; Dobson Books Ltd for extract on p. 28 from *The Four Routes* by Le Corbusier, quoted in *Faith of an Artist* by J. Wilson; Columbia University Press for extract on p. 32 from *The Long Revolution* by Raymond Williams; Williams & Norgat Ltd for extracts on pp. 35, 53 and 54 from *Style and Idea* by A. Schoenberg; on p. 36, extract from *For a New Novel: Essays on Fiction* by Alain Robbe-Grillet, transl. by Richard Howard, (c) 1965 by Grove Press, Inc. Published by Grove Press, Inc.; on p. 36, extract from *Snapshots* by Alain Robbe-Grillet, transl. by Bruce Morrissette, copyright (c) 1968 by Grove Press, Inc. Published by Grove Press Inc.; on pp. 39, 40, 56, 65, 66 and 123, extracts from *Henry Moore on Sculpture* edited by Philip James, copyright (c) Philip James and Henry Moore 1966. All rights reserved. Reprinted by permission of The Viking Press, Inc.; Penguin Books Ltd for extracts on

91, extract from *Collected Poems* by Wilfred Owen. Copyright Chatto & Windus, Ltd 1946, (c) 1963. Reprinted by permission of New Directions Publishing Corporation, New York; Alfred A. Knopf, Inc. for extracts on pp. 92, 93, 113, 119 and 120 from *The Death of Tragedy* by George Steiner; on pp. 98 and 99, extracts from *The Metamorphosis of the Gods* by André Malraux, copyright (c) 1960 by André Malraux. Reprinted by permission of Doubleday & Co. Inc.; Charles Scribner's Sons for extract on p. 100 from *The Conflict of Religions* by Philip H. Ashby; Professor Claude Lévi-Strauss and George Steiner for extract on p. 101 from 'A Conversation with Claude Lévi-Strauss' by George Steiner, in *Encounter*, April, 1966; Oxford University Press for extract on p. 101 from 'The Elegy of the Waters' by Léopold Sédar Senghor from *Prose and Poetry* by Léopold Sédar Senghor edited by J. Reed and C. Wake; *The Times Literary Supplement* for extract on p. 103 from 'Finding Their Voices', a special number of *The Times Literary Supplement*, September 16, 1965; on pp. 104 and 105, extracts from *A History of Chinese Literature* by Lai Ming, copyright (c) 1964 Lai Ming, reprinted by permission of The John Day Co. Inc., publisher; George Braziller, Inc. for extract on p. 107 from *Modern Architecture* by Vincent Scully, Jr.; on pp. 108 and 109 extracts from *Things Fall Apart* (c) 1959 by Chinua Achebe, reprinted by permission of Astor-Honor, Inc., New York; Mrs E. V. Eliot and Faber and Faber Ltd for extract on p. 112 from T. S. Eliot's review of Joyce's Ulysses in *The Dial*; on p. 114, extract from 'Sonnet to Orpheus' by Rainer Maria Rilke, from *Selected Works, II*, transl. by J. B. Leishman, (c) The Hogarth Press, Ltd, 1960, reprinted by permission of New Directions Publishing Corporation, New York; on p. 114, extract from *The Complete Poems of D. H. Lawrence*, Vol. II, edited by Vivian De Sola Pinto and F. Warren Roberts. Copyright 1933, by Frieda Lawrence. All rights reserved. Reprinted by permission of The Viking Press, Inc.; on p. 117, extract from *Duino Elegies* by Rainer Maria Rilke, transl. by J. B. Leishman and Stephen Spender, copyright (c) 1939 by W. W. Norton & Co. Inc. Copyright renewed (c) 1967 by J. B. Leishman and Stephen Spender; Alfred A. Knopf for extract on p. 118 from *Dr. Faustus* by Thomas Mann, transl. by H. T. Lowe-Porter; on p. 125, extract from *The Theatre of the Absurd* by Martin Esslin, copyright (c) 1961 by Martin Esslin, reprinted by per-

extract on p. 202 from *ESP: A Personal Memoir* by Rosalind Heywood; the Hibbert Trust for extract on p. 203 from *Hibbert Journal*, Vol. 47, by Professor H. Price.

The authors and publishers are grateful to the following for permission to reproduce the illustrations used in this book: J. Allan Cash Ltd (3); The Museum of Modern Art, New York (4); Contemporary Films (5); Daiei Motion Picture Co. Ltd, Tokyo (6); Gerda Goedhart & Helene Weigel (7); Martha Swope (9); Bargate Films Ltd (10); Herr Heinz Köster (12).

While all due effort has been made to contact copyright holders, the authors and publishers have been unable to do so in every case.

The Bibliographies

BIBLIOGRAPHICAL references are given at the end of each chapter. All such references are to editions used by the authors. Where a title is available from a U.S. publisher as well as from the English publisher given the entry has been marked by an asterisk. Page references are to the editions given.

ART

David W. Bolam

Introduction

THE new is disturbing. It may be feared as a threat to what a man enjoys, to a life in which he finds security and meaning, or the new may be welcomed for its excitement and release, and bring with it a great charge of hope. Most of us know both responses. The modern world is unavoidably new. Skyscraper and super-jet, Einstein and Freud, Communist China, and African leaders at U.N.E.S.C.O., great healing and dreaded annihilation. Yeats, writing of the Irish Rising of 1916, used a phrase which has meaning for this wider context:

> 'All changed, changed utterly:
> A terrible beauty is born.'[1]

Terror and beauty have disturbed men before, especially in their experience of the creative arts—in the presence of Oedipus, for example, old and blind, or of Lear carrying the dead body of Cordelia. Yet the disturbance of art can also be felt in the surprise of a melody, the leap of a dance, the startling beauty of a vase. The laughter of the wine and the destructive frenzy, comedy and tragedy, were fused in the god of the theatre, Dionysus. For all art knows creative excitement, the agitation of making something new, and those who enjoy such things are shaken, even if ever so slightly, so that they are forced to look at life afresh.

If, then, the art of all time, and the modern world, both contain an element that attracts, repels, and refuses to leave one indifferent, what of modern art? Many comments have been hurled at it: 'disgusting', 'primitive', 'obscene', 'a child could have done it', 'verbal diarrhoea', 'gloomy', 'sick', 'violent', 'whatever does it mean?', 'just a ghastly noise'. For all their crudity these comments are important, if only as clues to a problem. They show disappointment: a resentment that art has not offered what people expected

and felt they needed. They show disgust at having been hit 'below
the belt', but also fascination with that region. They show a be-
wilderment so severe as to suggest a breakdown of communication between public and artist.

All these issues will need fuller discussion, but two further
questions are also raised of so wide a scope as to provide the twin
structure of this section. First, the question: 'Is it art at all?'
Behind this lies a head-on clash between the public and contemporary artists as to what art is all about. This is discussed in Part
One: The Dispute: The Conflict Between Producer and Con-
sumer. Secondly, the question: 'Is this really the twentieth-
century world?' Looking at the horrors of modern art, the public
hopes against hope that these are not a fair description of the
world in which they live and work. This problem is examined in
Part Two: The Search: Exploring Contemporary Reality.

For the moment, three protests against modern art need a brief
glance, if only to avoid some misunderstanding. First, there is
the accusation that it is degenerate. No less figures than Hitler
and Khrushchev have said so. 'But', as a Jewish thinker warns us,
'let us be careful! We are speaking of ourselves. If this art is
degenerate, we too are degenerate, for innumerable individuals
are suffering the same collapse of the cultural canon, the same
alienation, the same loneliness—the rising blackness with its
shadow and devouring dragon. The disintegration and dissonance
of this art are our own; to understand them is to understand ourselves.'[2]

A second complaint follows that modern art is extremely depressing. To the same writer this is less than half the truth. The
totality of modern art, he asserts, 'in all its vast diversity, unfolds
around a mysterious centre, which as chaos and blackness, is
pregnant with a new doom, but also with a new world. In the
Duino Elegies Rilke wrote:

"... For Beauty's nothing
   but beginning of Terror we're still just able to bear,
   and why we adore it so is because it serenely
   disdains to destroy us. ..."

More than to any other beauty in art, these words apply to the
terrible beauty of modern art, which itself denies that it is beauty.
Never before was the beautiful so close to the terrible.'[3]

The third line of attack is that modern art is disunited—a chaotic outpouring, with each man for himself. This raises a practical point and a general one. The practical point is the difficulty raised throughout this book by using the words 'art' and 'artist' to cover the whole field of creative activity, whereas popular usage recognizes no such unity, and limits these words to the visual arts. One can only ask the reader to keep his wits awake, and adapt remarks where necessary. The general point, however, is fundamental. Does there really exist, has there ever been, such an entity as art—'ARS UNA'? It is a question to bear in mind continuously.

A glance at dates will not provide an answer, but a suggestive starting point. Yeats' words on a 'terrible beauty' were published in 1921; Rilke's on 'Beauty . . . beginning of Terror' appeared in 1923. The year in between, 1922, saw the publishing of Eliot's 'The Waste Land' and Joyce's *Ulysses*, as well as Le Corbusier's exhibition *Ville Contemporaine*, with its plan for a city of three million inhabitants. During these same years, Chaplin was gaining world popularity; Paris was watching ballets which exploited such diverse talents as Picasso, Stravinsky, and Diaghilev; skyscrapers were thrusting higher and higher in an America famed for gangsters and jazz; Klee and Kandinsky were busy at the Bauhaus and Schoenberg was completing his first atonal work, based on a twelve-tone sequence. Nor is it irrelevant that in 1923, for example, Hitler attempted a rising in Munich, Gandhi was in prison, Lenin was dying and Russian communists were advising the Kuomintang in China. All this does not prove that the arts are one, but it does suggest a very remarkable interaction between them in response to a very disturbed world.

REFERENCES

1. YEATS, W. B.: *Selected Poetry* (St. Martins Library. Macmillan, 1962). From the poem 'Easter 1916'.*
2. NEUMANN, E.: *Art and the Creative Unconscious*, tr. R. Manheim (Routledge, 1959). From the essay 'Art and Time', p. 121.*
3. NEUMANN: op. cit., p. 133. For the Rilke quotation, see RILKE, R. M.: *Selected Poems*. Introduced and translated by J. B. Leishman (Penguin Modern European Poets, 1964). From the First Elegy.*

PART ONE

THE DISPUTE

THE CONFLICT BETWEEN CONSUMER AND PRODUCER

CHAPTER ONE

What Society Hopes For

IF an interviewer had pressed some Victorians with the question, 'What do you expect an artist to do?', it is possible that four ideas of the artist might have emerged. One view would have seen the artist as an illustrator, a man who provides society with a record of people, events or experiences, in terms which they can easily assimilate and recognize, and which will ensure that a record is passed on to future generations. Another view would have wanted the artist to be a visionary, a man of exceptional insight, who saw deeper into the meaning of things than other men, and expressed himself with almost uncomfortable intensity. More appealing would be the wish for the artist to be a decorator, one who added a beauty to everyday life by the creation of pleasing forms, balanced and harmonious. Lastly, some might have seen the artist as something of a magician, a man capable of producing a heightened awareness and excitement of the senses.

Illustrator, visionary, decorator, magician. Such expectations could be appropriate to the work of any artist in any medium. Certainly, the nineteenth century wanted illustration not only from the portrait, landscape, or still-life, but also from the narrative and character-drawing of the novel, opera, and programmed music. Visionary art was not just the work of poet or essayist; a painter or composer of choral music should equally inspire with their view of life. Nor was it only the sculptor or interior designer who were decorators; mellifluous symphonies also added the desired grace to life. And a creator's magic could be enjoyed just as well in colour, or in a haunting melody, or the cadence of a lyric.

A concept of a rôle, however, contains ideas of how an artist works and the qualities he should have. If one regards him as an illustrator, one is likely to stress his skill at creating illusion, and one will judge him for his fidelity to nature, or conformity to a

21

view-point. The visionary artist, probably thought of as a strange outsider, will be assessed for his sensitivity and originality. He may be thought of as an instrument, who becomes inspired by some force greater than himself. For the decorator, the emphasis will be on craftsmanship, with a stress on his good taste and on harmonious form rather than content. Virtuosity will be encouraged. As for the artist-magician, the basic demand will be for the sensuous, and for the kind of emotive power that lies beyond the immediate meaning of the work. In the past, it was an easy step to believe that he had contact with the supernatural.

Thought of a further past suggests that these ideas may be older and of more universality than simply as wishes of nineteenth-century Europeans. The Mogul emperors wanted miniaturists, for instance, to provide an illustrative record of their dynasty, and the medieval popes wanted the artist to express the world-picture of their church. The Hebrew prophets were visionary artists, and Cassandra was honoured in Homer. The Chinese potter would have understood decoration as a life ideal, and Mozart wrote music to embellish gracious living. As for the 'magic' of the artist—a cliché for the Victorians—perhaps here are the strangest roots of all; a blend of the sensuous and the religious, pointing to Hindu temples, the masks and dances of Africa, the music of the mass, with more than a hint of Dionysus.

A record, social and moral understanding, beauty, an experience of the divine; these are some of the things which men in the past and not least the Victorians wanted to be given by art.

I. THE SHAKING OF THE FOUNDATIONS

'He stumbles, no, he has flung himself down, a hell-hound is coming howling, a huge explosive shell, a disgusting sugar-loaf from the infernal regions. He lies with his face in the cool mire, legs sprawled out, feet twisted, heels turned down. . . . Farewell, honest Hans Castorp, farewell . . . and if thou livest or diest! Thy prospects are poor. The desperate dance, in which thy fortunes are caught up, will last yet many a sinful year; we should not care to set a high stake on thy life by the time it ends . . .'[1]

Hans Castorp had left *The Magic Mountain* and returned to the flat-land, only to find that the flat-land had become the grisly battlefield of the First World War. His creator, Thomas Mann, saw this as one more symptom of the decay of European civilization. Spengler had just published *The Decline of the West*. Opinions over these diagnoses will differ, but a feeling of having left some comfortable Victorian resort was widespread, and it seems fair to ask whether their ideas of art could any longer be viable in the changed world of the twentieth century.

If an artist is to be an illustrator, then he and his public must share a belief in, and a way of looking at, his subjects—material things, people, the flow of events. Few things, however, have received a sharper knock than our ideas about the physical world. Max Planck was right when he said that the quantum theory was to 'play a fundamental role in physics, heralding the advent of a new state of things, destined, perhaps, to transform completely our physical concepts which have been founded upon the assumption of the continuity of all causal chains of events'.[2] Even if the layman understands little of all this, or of Einstein's theory of relativity, or of Heisenberg's uncertainty principle, or of the physics of nuclear fission, none the less a sense of disturbance is felt. The visual artists, in particular, were bound to respond. 'In my mind,' wrote Kandinsky in 1912, 'the collapse of the atom was the collapse of the whole world: suddenly the stoutest walls fell. Everything turned unstable, insecure or soft. I would not have been surprised if a stone had melted into thin air before my eyes. Science seemed to have been annihilated.' And, as he later added, 'It seemed as if I saw art steadily disengaging itself from nature.'[3]

If art disengaged itself from nature, it was also forced to disengage itself from a view of man, for Freud had exploded a comparable depth charge. Man was not what he seemed. 'Mental processes', claimed Freud, 'are essentially unconscious, and those which are conscious are merely isolated acts and parts of the whole psychic entity.' Moreover, the sexual impulses 'play a peculiarly large part' and have 'contributed invaluably to the highest cultural, artistic, and social achievements of the human mind'.[4] Though continually challenged, Freud's ideas have become so widespread that Auden could write at his death in 1939:

'. . . If often he was wrong and at times absurd;
To us he is no more a person
Now but a whole climate of opinion.'[5]

After Freud artists could not continue just to record appearances, to say nothing of the fact that what with cameras, X-rays,
tapes and the rest, modern technology could provide a fuller,
more exact, more instant record of man and his doings than the
artists ever had.

If the illustrators had been shown to have only an 'insubstantial
pageant', the visionaries were left with a 'baseless fabric', for the
base of vision is a belief in individual man. Both the individual's
ability to understand events and his significance within them were
now to be challenged. Where Freud left off, Marx and Frazer took
over. And where the theorists left off, the hard facts of modern
industrial living intruded. Out of European life came Ortega y
Gasset's *The Revolt of the Masses*; out of America, Mumford's
The Culture of Cities, Riesman's *The Lonely Crowd*, and Whyte's
The Organization Man. No wonder that Herzog, at a tense moment of his story, could reflect:

'. . . What it means to be a man. In a city. In transition. In a
mass. Transformed by science. Under organized power. Subject to enormous controls. In a condition caused by mechaniza-
tion. After the late failure of radical hopes. In a society that
was no community and devalued the person. Owing to the
multiplied power of numbers which made the self negligible.
Which spent military billions against foreign enemies but
would not pay for order at home. Which permitted savagery
and barbarism in its own great cities . . .'[6]

Herzog's creator, Saul Bellow, had more to say on this theme
on another occasion:

'. . . The First World War with its millions of corpses gave
an aspect of the horrible to romantic over-valuation of the Self.
The leaders of the Russian Revolution were icy in their hatred
of bourgeois individualism. In the Communist countries millions were sacrificed in the building of socialism, and almost
certainly the Lenins and the Stalins, the leaders who made the
decisions, serving the majority and the future, believed they
were rejecting a soft, nerveless humanism which attempted

in the face of natural and historical evidence to oppose progress.

'A second great assault on the separate Self sprang from Germany. . . . Just what the reduction of millions of human beings into heaps of bone and mounds of rag and hair or clouds of smoke betokened, there is no one who can plainly tell us, but it is at least plain that something was being done to put in question the meaning of survival, the meaning of pity, the meaning of justice and of the importance of being oneself, the individual's consciousness of his own existence.'[7]

Amid such desperate ugliness the role of the decorator—the artist as creator of beauty—is clearly made more difficult. One can gain some measure of the disturbance by asking whether lyric poetry is still possible. Is poetry still possible, for instance, when just below the surface apparently man is a chaos of twisted desires? D. H. Lawrence vented his irritation against Heine's love lyric:

> 'Thou art like a flower,
>   So chaste and lovely and pure. . . .'[8]

Again, is lyric poetry possible in an urban civilization, where 'no birds sing'? Once more a somewhat shrill Lawrence suggests 'No':

> 'The real tragedy of England . . . is the tragedy of ugliness . . . the great crime which the moneyed classes and promoters of industry committed in the palmy Victorian days was the condemning of the workers to ugliness, ugliness, ugliness: meanness and formless and ugly surroundings, ugly ideals, ugly religion, ugly hope, ugly love, ugly clothes, ugly furniture, ugly homes, ugly relationship between workers and employers. . . .'[9]

Yet again, is lyric poetry possible in the world of the concentration camps? Brecht raised doubts:

> 'Whatever times are these, when a chat about trees is almost a crime, because it means being silent over so many wrongs!'[10]

And Camus was even more outspoken:

> '. . . One cannot enjoy the cry of birds in the coolness of the evening—the world such as it is. For now it is covered by a

thick layer of history which its language must penetrate to reach us. It is deformed by it. Nothing in it is felt for itself because to the world's every moment is joined a whole series of images of death or despair. There are no more mornings without agonies, no more evenings without prisons and no more noons without fearful slaughter.'[11]

The issue at the moment, however, is less with the future of poetry than with the necessity forced upon contemporary man of re-examining, enlarging, perhaps rejecting, traditional ideas of beauty. We know too much on earth to declare that 'Beauty is truth, truth beauty'.

Twentieth-century man had not only left his 'magic casements' because he found the view ugly, but also because he was ceasing to believe in magic. By early in this century, the word 'magic' might be found in one of two contexts: either in the thought-world of Frazer's *Golden Bough* and Freud's *Totem and Taboo*, or in the excessive claims of advertisers and popular entertainers. In short, it suggested either the primitive or the trivial. This reflects an undermining of two basic aspects of 'magic' power in art: the power of order, as known in ritual and ceremony, and the power of the sensuous. These are, of course, not separate factors. Ritual can be heightened by the sensuous, and the sensuous can be enriched by awe; whereas both are weakened by a breakdown of religious belief. Leaving that breakdown for examination in the second part of this book, it is necessary to probe further the distrust of the sensuous, for the sensuous in the past has been thought of as fundamental to art: its power to appeal to deeper levels, and the basis of a group experience.

Just there, however, the rot may have begun, for depths and the group have been exploited by dictators. One thinks of Hitler with his mass rallies, and his cynical claim that:

> 'The broad masses of a nation are always more easily corrupted in the deeper strata of their emotional nature, than consciously or voluntarily.'[12]

The sensuous could become, it seems, the fanaticism of the Nazis, and poor Wagner, now open to criticism for artistic excess, became associated with an inflated racialism. Such is the situation of Yeats' much-quoted lines:

'. . . Things fall apart; the centre cannot hold;
Mere anarchy is loosed upon the world,
The blood-dimmed tide is loosed, and everywhere
The ceremony of innocence is drowned;
The best lack all conviction, while the worst
Are full of passionate intensity.'[13]

If such things showed a 'corruption of the deeper emotional strata' this was only to reinforce doubts raised by Freud: is the non-rational side of man to be trusted? Yet it is in the non-rational side of man—feeling, intuition, the senses—that the sensuous has its roots. Industrial society further increases the difficulty. Large impersonal organizations, the privacies of suburban living, the necessity of highly trained intelligence, the demand for expertise in a limited area of knowledge, the prestige given to the technological, the hygienic safeguards from the natural—all take men further away from a pattern of life when the sensuous had earth-roots:

'. . . the brown god is almost forgotten
By the dwellers in cities . . .'[14]

This is not to foreclose on the future, and deny the possibility of new patterns: it is only to stress that the modern artist has been under heavy bombardment. He has lived among ruins.

'What are the roots that clutch, what branches grow
Out of this stony rubbish? Son of man,
You cannot say, or guess, for you know only
A heap of broken images, where the sun beats,
And the dead tree gives no shelter, the cricket no relief,
And the dry stone no sound of water. . . .'[15]

2. A BONUS FOR BOTH SIDES

All the same, artists are busy. Indeed, for the lucky ones art is big business. Whatever shaking the modern world has given the artist, and however sharply contemporaries may assess his work, there is a vast amount of art in all media being produced. Many artists are as shrewd as any industrialist in exploiting the possibilities which the twentieth century offers them. At the very least, they have been offered four hard gains.

First, and most obvious, are the gifts of technology: a new art form—the motion picture, the widest of screens and the glossiest of colours; and extended resources, so that architects, for instance, can plan buildings rising high on narrow pillars, with all the delights of plate-glass, plastics and chromium. Some of the 'de-lights' may be questioned. Hollywood may offer strange gods and New York disturb, as it disturbed an African poet:

> '. . . the anguish in the depth of skyscraper streets
> Lifting eyes hawkhooded to the sun's eclipse.
> Sulphurous your light and livid the towers with heads that
>   thunderbolt the sky
> The skyscrapers which defy the storms with muscles of
>   steel and stone-glazed hide. . . .'[16]

Yet the film and the steel-concrete building are of the greatest importance to the modern arts. For one thing, they show the co-operation instead of the hostility of the arts and the technical sciences. As Pevsner said of the designer of the Bauhaus:

> 'It is the creative energy of this world in which we live and work and which we want to master, a world of science and technique, of speed and danger, of hard struggles and no per-sonal security, that is glorified in Gropius' architecture.'[17]

No group of artists show such enthusiasm as the architects:

> 'To visit a dam', wrote Le Corbusier, 'in the course of con-struction gives one a feeling of exhilaration—it is an essentially modern concept of power. . . . Show us the back of a dam, to which are fixed spirals of turbines. There is nothing more lovely, vaster, nearer to those great laws of nature which we see reflected not only in fir-cones and sea-shells but in the calyx of a flower, the anatomy of an insect.'[18]

Both architecture and film-making, moreover, are co-operative arts, involving a team of both technicians and designers. Such an idealism inspired the Bauhaus; and Cocteau wrote with warmth:

> 'I've never yet come across a film director who, speaking of his unit did not affirm, "It's the best there is". This brings me

back to the idea of a family . . . akin to the family of antiquity, bound by a common interest, and by that affectionate attachment which grows from contact.'[19]

Again, these two arts are essentially world-wide, as will be shown later. They help to fructify other arts. Sculptor and interior designer have been given new scope by the architect; while the composer has often worked closely with the film director, as did Prokofiev with Eisenstein on *Alexander Nevsky*. Lastly, they have helped break the arts away from a limiting sense of being a luxury for a leisured class. One of Le Corbusier's buildings was a massive block of working-class flats at Marseilles, and the cinema is probably the world's most popular art form. Charlie Chaplin, it has been said, is the folk hero of an age of mass democracy.

Mass audiences in themselves might be regarded as the second hard gain for the modern artist. Never before in the history of man has it been possible for the work of a single artist to reach so large an audience, in so many different parts of the world, with every hope that such an audience will be educated, and perhaps, receptive enough to enjoy it. Recorded TV and radio programmes, touring theatre and dance companies, films, gramophone records, paperbacks, art reproductions, all have a world market. Not all such material is good, or even modern; nor would one want to defend art on the same graph as sales value, but it would be absurd to deny that one of the great strengths of modern art is its availability and universality.

If art is available to a wider public, it is also available to the artists themselves, and this represents a third major gain. There is no longer any need for an artist to be locked in one tradition because he is unaware of the work of his contemporaries, or indeed of any age. The modern artist has every chance to study art forms from every part of the world, and of societies at every stage of development, from the primitive to the most sophisticated. It remains to be seen whether this has provided something of the stimulus which the sixteenth-century discoveries may have given to Shakespeare and his contemporaries.

The last gain is more general but equally important: an understanding of process. Probably out of the sense that our society is a rapidly changing one, a good deal of scrutiny has been given to

the creative process by psychologists, sociologists, and philosophers. One potential advantage of this for the artist is that such
thinking may give him understanding and support in a line of
experiment, which he has arrived at independently by his own
searchings. To give one example: Worringer and abstract art. In
1906 Wilhelm Worringer published his book *Abstraction and
Empathy*. In it he argued that man has always felt the need for
self-alienation. One way of doing this was by empathy: 'To enjoy
aesthetically means to enjoy myself in a sensuous object diverse
from myself, to empathize myself into it.' The other way was
through abstraction: the deliverance of oneself from chaos by
ordering the inanimate, from 'the fortuitousness of humanity as
a whole, from the seeming arbitrariness of organic existence in
general, in the contemplation of something necessary and irre-
fragable'.[20] Here, even before the movement was launched, is
philosophic defence of one of the most interesting areas of modern
art. At the same time, such thinking was not only open to help
the artist in his work, it could also be used to clarify the 'meaning'
of his work to a bewildered public. Such a public might not, of
course, read Worringer directly. More likely, his ideas would
come to them through a perceptive critic, or probably through
one of the talks, TV programmes and paperbacks which are
some of their biggest cuts in the bonus of modernity.

3. SOCIETY RE-EXAMINES ITS DEMANDS

All these changes may have been disturbing or exhilarating, but
had they caused society to change its demands from the artist?
Or did society want the same things from the artist as had previous generations? Whatever they wanted, did the pressure of
society really determine what the artists did? One difficulty, and
perhaps itself a sign of a changed situation, is that of defining
'society'. At times one will mean the State, at others the widest
possible audience who enjoy mass media, or just that section who
read the 'posh Sundays', or even the small group of influential
critics. Generally, it is a definition by use: namely the people who
will actually go to modern exhibitions, read modern novels, listen
to modern music. But this only conceals another difficulty; not all
the art which is being produced today can be called 'modern'.

Indeed, probably the greater part of the best-selling novels, musicals, West End comedies, sculptured busts of local dignitaries, and coloured reproductions for drawing-room walls may have been produced in the twentieth century, but are not the kind of modern art which forms the subject of this book. This fact in itself suggests a formidable continuity with the artistic tastes and wishes of a previous century. It would be interesting to probe the situation further and look for the pockets of 'modernity' in this majority taste—perhaps many contemporary textile designs would offer an example.

One cannot avoid a side glance, however, at this whole concept of 'majority taste' with the accusations made against it that such art is second rate and escapist. Before joining issue one might usefully force oneself to assess artists whose work was widely popular, at any rate for a time, and which received definite, if divided, praise from the critics. What is *your* opinion, for example, of the writings of Charles Morgan, Graham Greene, Christopher Fry, Dylan Thomas, or John Betjeman? One could also scrutinize the whole process of the formation of public taste, and explore the significance of the programme divisions of the B.B.C. Not least one could look at such loaded words as 'high-brow', 'egg-head', 'the masses', 'popular entertainment'.

Such words are no more than random shots in the crucial debate about the place of the arts in our society, between those who defend the idea of an élite culture and those who uphold that of a common culture for all. In England, one of the most aggressive supporters of the élite view has been F. R. Leavis who wrote:

'In any period it is upon a very small minority that the discerning appreciation of art and literature depends: it is (apart from cases of the simple and familiar) only a few who are capable of unprompted, first-hand judgement. They are still a small minority, though a larger one, who are capable of endorsing such first-hand judgement by genuine personal response. The accepted valuations are a kind of paper currency based upon a very small proportion of gold. To the state of such a currency the possibilities of fine living at any time bear a close relation.'[21]

With an equal concern for 'fine living' but with a contrasting

emphasis, Raymond Williams wrote in discussing the creative
mind that:

> 'Communication is the process of making unique experi-
> ence into common experience, and it is, above all, the claim to
> live. For what we basically say, in any kind of communication,
> is: "I am living in this way because this is my experience". The
> ability to live in a particular way depends, ultimately, on
> acceptance of this experience by others, in successful communi-
> cation. Thus our descriptions of our own experience come to
> compose a network of relationships, and all our communica-
> tion systems, including the arts, are literally part of our social
> organizations.'[22]

So the debate goes on, made sharper at times by underlying
differences of opinion about those 'social organizations'. Some
supporters of an élite culture have been severe critics of industrial
society and nostalgic for organic rural communities. Some supporters of a common culture have been political idealists of the
Left, and may have seen in Soviet Russia proof of their thesis,
somewhat in the spirit of Khrushchev's boast:

> 'We are living at a time when literature and art, as Lenin
> predicted, have become an integral part of the cause of the
> whole people.'[23]

Communism, however, prompts a return to questions raised
at the start, whether society now makes changed demands of the
artist. For Soviet art offers a surprisingly pure example of continuity of the illustrator-artist tradition, in this case to illustrate
the world view of Russian Communism. It is entirely consistent
with this view that the art-language should be popular—'socialist
realism'—and that the photographic approach should underline
a materialist philosophy. To Western eyes, however, it is a weakness, and unexpected evidence of continuity, that it should seem
so Victorian, expecially in the visual arts—naturalistic, didactic,
even prudish. Luckily that is not the whole story. Soviet Russia
has been highly successful in the art-form which has kept closest
to the illustrator tradition—the film. It was all the Russian leaders
could want: born, like their own revolution, in the twentieth
century, as technical as a tractor, offering photographic realism,
popular in its appeal and capable of reaching wide audiences in

village and city. Not least, it could convey a message which could be understood by the illiterate. From such a prosaic starting-point, Dovzhenko, Pudovkin, and above all, Eisenstein, have made films of poetic excitement.

Thus a great measure of continuity has been found in majority art, whether the commercial art of London or the state art of Moscow. There has, however, been a pressure for continuity, which has probably impinged more sharply on the modern artist. The pressure points are on art as visionary and magico-religious: an increasing wish for the artist to serve as priest, psychiatrist, and political thinker. Where need is real, and traditional aids have broken down, all this is very understandable, but from the artist's viewpoint it is excessive. Such a demand asks him to be something which he is not, distracts him from technical problems with its concern with content, and often probes into the strains and pains of his private personality. 'The artist', as a critic angrily suggested, has been given 'the role of a huckster amusing that small sophisticated section of the public who are queueing up in their own furry night for their own personal salvation via Culture'.[24]

At the same time, this pressure may be a valuable stimulus to the artist to drive back to forgotten elements; to a religious art, for instance, that knows more of Dionysus than did the effete gothic of the nineteenth century. An unexpected shout of approval may come from a group outside both—the 'enfants terribles' of teen-age pop culture. In their anger against society they may find a sympathetic echo in the anger of the artist.

4. THE ANGER OF THE ARTIST

One thing that always angers the artist is for society to suggest that he has a certain rôle to carry out. What particularly angers a modern artist is that he should be expected to carry out rôles that were the fashion in the nineteenth century. For he is anti-representation, anti-inspiration, anti-message, anti-values, anti-beauty, anti-narrative, anti-sensuous, anti-perspective, anti-harmony, anti-'purple-patch'. More than anything else, he is against his immediate predecessors.

Why this hostility? Because to follow his predecessors' conventions and attitudes would block his own growth. Why, then, not just put their work on one side, and start working in a new way? Because public opinion's concept of art is still that of the artists of at least a generation ago. So the modern artist finds himself forced to fight his audiences, so that he can be free to do some essential re-thinking. Ironically, at the very point in history when larger audiences seem to be open to the artist than ever before, artists find a need to attack all their conceptions of art. Hence the full debate, of which the 'high-brow'—'mass culture' controversy is only one strand. Strangely, the artist, in an age of mass communications, is often a solitary figure, and on the defensive.

Anger and attack, however, imply that the artists have their own objectives. A basic one is to reconquer their own medium, and to separate it both from other media and from external demands. A painter wants to be a painter; a musician, a musician. This is not from any feeling of hostility to the other arts, or empire-building for its own sake. Nor does it mean that artists are against such fruitful co-operation as that of Cocteau and Stravinsky in *Oedipus Rex*, or that offered by film and architecture, as already mentioned. What they are against are mongrels like the painting *When did you last see your father?* Even more they are against art masquerading as philosophy or religion. In the face of such a demand, artists are often deflating of themselves. When challenged at the frontier, for instance, Stravinsky said he was an "inventor of music". 'The gendarme, then verifying my passport, asked me why I was listed as composer. I told him that the expression "inventor of music" seemed to me to fit my profession more exactly than the term applied to me in the documents authorizing me to cross borders.'[25]

It was not enough, of course, just to separate out his own medium; the artist had to explore the possibilities of that medium to the limit, and so re-conquer it, and know its full power. So modern painters, for instance, in exploring their medium have often concentrated on abstract art: pictures, that is, where the whole experience is in the forms and the colours, and with no attempt at representation. Consumers may protest that all they are being offered are technical experiments. In a sense that is true. But artists are increasingly inclined to retort that the medium says all; indeed that it could only be said in that way. The meaning is all in the paint, or the sounds, or the words. As Schoenberg said:

> 'I had completely understood the Schubert songs, together with their poems, from the music alone, and the poems of Stefan George, from their sound alone, with a perfection that by analysis and synthesis could not have been attained.'

And he noted with approval that when:

> '. . . Wassily Kandinsky and Oskar Kokoschka paint pictures the objective theme of which is hardly more than an excuse to improvise in colours and forms and to express themselves as only the musician expressed himself until now, these are symptoms of a gradually expanding knowledge of the true nature of art.' (1912)[26]

Six years earlier, a character in a Shaw play had declared:

> 'I believe in Michael Angelo, Velasquez, and Rembrandt; in the might of design, the mystery of colour, the redemption of all things by Beauty everlasting, and the message of art that has made these hands blessed.'[27]

Modern artists would agree with the 'design' and the 'colour', for these are vital aspects of the medium concerned, but three other words would rouse their protest, and for a double reason: such ideas both cramp their own freedom of exploration, and also weaken art. One enemy word is 'Beauty'—not least with the capital B. One thinks of Gregory Corso's poem:

> '. . . The child trembled, fell,
>   and staggered up again,
>   *I screamed his name!*
>   And a fury of mothers and fathers
>   sank their teeth into his brain.
>   I called to the angels of my generation
>   on the rooftops, in the alleyways,
>   beneath the garbage and the stones,
>   *I screamed the name!* and they came
>   and gnawed the child's bones.
>   *I screamed the name: Beauty*
>   *Beauty Beauty Beauty.*'[28]

This is the other side of a penny already looked at. From the artist's view, the use of 'Beauty' as authoritative, limits both the range of his material, and his manner of handling it. Too often it will weaken art by wanting the ornamental, perhaps added irrelevantly as decoration on the outside. The harshness of life, basic forms, bold outlines make for power.

Another enemy idea is 'everlasting'. Modern artists, sharply aware of their society, insist that circumstances and values change, and so must art forms. To do otherwise condemns art to a perpetual series of imitations, all pseudo-Greek or whatever the approved eternal form may be. It weakens the chance of something gaunt and new emerging, with all the demands that it would make on the sensibility. As Mahler said: 'Tradition is slovenliness.'

And the last enemy word is 'message'. As one defender of the French 'new novel' said:

'Before the work there is nothing: no certainty, no purpose, no message. To believe that the novelist has "something to say", and that he then tries to discover how to say it, is the gravest misconception. For it is precisely this "how", this way of saying things, that constitutes the whole, obscure project of the writer and that later becomes the dubious content of his book.'[29]

There is more disagreement here, but many other artists would say that their art comes first and not any social purpose. For one thing, they would argue, a 'noble' message can become an excuse for shoddy art, just as a 'beautiful' container could justify its emptiness. Their stress is that form and content are inseparable, just like a tiger and his skin.

So, not without anger, modern artists have tried to clear the ground for their own work and for a more powerful art. But each artist now faced a problem: the burden of creation was on his shoulders alone. What André Malraux said of the painters could be adapted for all:

'No longer made to tell a story, the world seen by the artist was transmuted into painting; the apples of a still life were not glorified apples but glorified colour. And the crucial discovery was made that, in order to become painting, the universe seen by the artist had to become a private one, created by himself.'[30]

REFERENCES

1. MANN, T.: *The Magic Mountain* (Secker and Penguin). From the closing paragraphs.*
2. PLANCK, M.: *Nobel Prize Address, 1920*. Quoted from MOULTON and SCHIFFERES (eds.): *The Autobiography of Science* (New York: Doubleday, 1945), p. 540.
3. KANDINSKY, W.: Quoted from JUNG, C. G.: *Man and his Symbols* (Aldus Books, 1964), p. 262, in the illuminating essay by Aniela Jaffé—'Symbolism in the Visual Arts': a rich source for the artists' own comments on their work.*
4. FREUD, S.: *Introductory Lectures on Psycho-analysis*. Tr. by Joan Riviere, and with a preface by Ernest Jones (Allen & Unwin, 2nd ed. 1929), pp. 16, 17.*
5. AUDEN, W. H.: *Another Time* (Faber, 1940), p. 116. From the poem 'In Memory of Sigmund Freud'.*
6. BELLOW, S.: *Herzog* (Weidenfeld & Nicolson, 1965), p. 201. Now available in Penguin Books.
7. BELLOW, S.: 'Some Notes on Recent American Fiction', in *Encounter*, November 1963, Vol. XXI, No. 5, pp. 22–3.
8. LAWRENCE, D. H.: *Sex, Literature and Censorship*. Edited by H. T. Moore (Heinemann, 1955), pp. 211–12.* For the Heine poem see *The Penguin Book of German Verse*, p. 327; the lyric begins
        'Du bist wie eine Blume,
        So hold und schön und rein. . . .'
9. LAWRENCE, D. H.: *Selected Essays* (Penguin, 1950).* From the essay 'Nottingham and the Mining Country', p. 119. The same passage is quoted and discussed in WILLIAMS, R.: *Culture and Society, 1780–1950* (Chatto & Windus, 1958).* See Penguin edition, p. 201
10. BRECHT, B.: *Gedichte und Lieder*. Selected by Peter Suhrkamp (Suhrkamp Verlag). From the poem 'An die Nachgeborenen, 1938' (To the Unborn), p. 158.
11. CAMUS, A.: *A Writer's Notebook*, tr. by A. Hartley, in *Encounter*, March 1965, Vol. XXIV, No. 3, p. 29.
12. HITLER, A.: *Mein Kampf*. Quoted from FIRTH, C. B.: *From Napoleon to Hitler* (London: Ginn, 1946), p. 380.
13. YEATS, W. B.: op. cit. From the poem 'The Second Coming'.
14. ELIOT, T. S.: *Four Quartets* (Faber, 1944. Also paperback). From 'The Dry Salvages'.*
15. ELIOT, T. S.: *Collected Poems 1909–1935* (Faber, 1936). From the opening section of 'The Waste Land'.*
16. SENGHOR, L. S.: Quoted from MOORE and BEIER (eds.): *Modern*

Poetry from Africa (Penguin African Library). From Senghor's poem 'New York—for jazz orchestra: trumpet solo', p. 51.*

17. PEVSNER, N.: *Pioneers of Modern Design* (Penguin, 1964), p. 217.*
18. LE CORBUSIER: *The Four Routes* (Dobson, 1948). Quoted from WILSON, J. (ed.): *Faith of an Artist* (Allen & Unwin, 1962), p. 215. This is a useful anthology of artists' personal statements.*
19. COCTEAU, J., and FRAIGNEAU, A.: *Cocteau on the Film* (Dobson, 1954), p. 57.*
20. WORRINGER, W.: *Abstraction and Empathy*, tr. by M. Bullock (Routledge, 1953), pp. 5, 24.*
21. LEAVIS, F. R.: *Mass Civilization and Minority Culture* (Cambridge, 1930), pp. 3–5. Quoted from WILLIAMS, R.: *Culture and Society*, op. cit., p. 247.
22. WILLIAMS, R.: *The Long Revolution* (Chatto & Windus, 1961).* Quoted here from the Penguin edition, p. 55.
23. KHRUSHCHEV, N.: From a speech in the Kremlin on March 8th, 1963, published as *Soviet Booklet No. 108*, p. 3.
24. BERGER, J.: Quoted from *Artist, Critic, and Teacher*—pamphlet of the Joint Council for Education through Art, London.
25. STRAVINSKY, I.: *Poetics of Music* (O.U.P., 1947), p. 53.*
26. SCHOENBERG, A.: *Style and Idea* (Williams & Norgate, 1951), pp. 4–5.
27. SHAW, G. B.: *The Doctor's Dilemma* (Constable Longmans, ed. A. C. WARD Penguin), Act IV.*
28. CORSO, G.: *Gasoline* (The Pocket Poets Series, No. 8, San Francisco, 1958). From the poem 'Don't Shoot the Warthog', p. 35.
29. ROBBE-GRILLET, A.: *Snapshots* and *Towards a New Novel* (in one volume, Calder, 1966. Tr. by Barbara Wright), p. 141.*
30. MALRAUX, A.: *The Voices of Silence*, tr. by S. Gilbert (Secker, 1954), p. 120.*

CHAPTER TWO

What the Artist Struggles For

WHY does the artist struggle to create at all? Out of his own distress? Many artists have said this:

'One puts into one's art what one has not been capable of putting into one's existence. It is because he was unhappy that God created the world.' (Montherlant)

'Art is for the artist sorrow, through which he frees himself for a further sorrow.' (Kafka)

'In life and painting I can quite well dispense with God. But, suffering as I am, I cannot dispense with something greater than myself, something that is my whole life: the power of creating.' (Van Gogh)[1]

Faced with the profound chaos of life, felt in his own person, the artist must create order. Forms, the essence of all art, are the achieving of order. But such forms are not just a tidying-up—the rationalizing mind can do that. They are not the solving of a jigsaw puzzle—each creation is always a new and unique answer. They are not just a personal prop for the artist—for a form is weak and without communication, unless it is supra-personal. Above anything else, the forms of art are power:

'Music is given us to establish an order in things; to order the chaotic and personal into something perfectly controlled, conscious and capable of lasting vitality.' (Stravinsky)[2]

'For me a work must have a vitality of its own. I do not mean a reflection of the vitality of life, of movement, of physical action, frisking, dancing figures and so on, but that a work can have in it a pent-up energy, an intense life of its own, independent of the object it may represent. When work has this powerful vitality we do not connect the word beauty with it. ...'

39

'. . . Between beauty of expression and power of expression
there is a difference of function. The first aims at pleasing the
senses, the second has a spiritual vitality which is for me more
moving and goes deeper than the senses.' (Moore)[3]

Faced with such powerful forms, the response of the onlooker,
reader, listener is an inevitable excitement. This excitement is
not passing, but lasting; continuing to work inside, raising new
questions, and giving a new sense of life:

'Before and above all, it is the visual shock that matters·
Afterwards, one wants to find out what it says, what it represents. But only afterwards.' (Miró)[4]

'For that thrill of excitement from our first reading of a work
of creative literature which we do not understand is itself the
beginning of understanding. . . . Understanding begins in the
sensibility: we must have the experience before we attempt to
explore the sources of the work itself.' (Eliot)[5]

'To explain away the mystery of a great painting—if such a
feat were possible—would do irreparable harm. . . . Mysteries
have to be respected if they are to retain their power. Art disturbs: Science reassures.' (Braque)[6]

And one of the most exciting mysteries is this fact: an experience
within the individual artist has, through his efforts, become a form
with a vital life of its own. Give it what meaning one will, secular
or personal, in this process the Word has become Flesh. As Yeats
said:

'I can entirely understand the excitement a god feels on getting
into a statue.'[7]

I. THE PROBLEM

'I can start on a task', wrote Cocteau, 'only if instead of having an
idea, an idea has me, and haunts, disturbs, torments me so un-
bearably that I am forced to get it out, to rid myself of it at any
cost. Thus work for me is a kind of torture.'[8] The process of idea
becoming form has always been recognized as a painful and testing one. Today there is the added difficulty that the traditional
techniques are of doubtful validity.

(a) *Detail and Framework*

The 'foretaste of the creative act accompanies the intuitive grasp of an unknown entity already possessed but not yet intelligible, an entity that will not take definite shape except by the action of a constantly vigilant technique'.[9]

But what is an artist's technique? Some idea may be gained by comparing the artist's use of detail and framework with that of other workers. An artist does not use details as would an administrator, concerned to keep a complete record, nor like a sociologist, analysing his data for trends; his use is both more fluid and more powerful. On the one hand, in art a detail changes its meaning according to its position in the whole, and in turn changes the significance of its neighbours—colours, tones, words; they all gain in force from each other, and from the activity—rhyme, colour pattern, counterpoint and the rest. On the other hand, a detail can sometimes do a wonder: it can stand for the whole. Just as the massacre on the Odessa steps can stand for the whole Russian Revolution, or Van Gogh's old boots show his experience of life. Both uses are forms of communication: the first is the language of the medium, the second symbolic language.

The same point could be made by looking at the use of a framework. An artist is not like a philosopher, who wants a logical plan, nor like a secretary making a précis of a meeting. The artist's framework is itself part of the meaning, of the communication. In a Mondrian painting, for example, the framework—the structuring of rectangles, lines and colours—is the experience. In Joyce's *Ulysses*, the myth is not just (as will be seen later) an organizing convenience; it also gives force and an extra significance to the story. Mondrian has relied entirely on the language of his medium; Joyce has called in symbolism.

The problem of the modern artist is that the technical language of his medium has run down, and that symbolism is under severe questioning. Hence Stravinsky's appeal for 'constant vigilance'.

(b) *The Language of the Medium*

One example will be used for all: the problem of words. Words—both spoken and written—have become debased. Mass society has overworked lyric language in selling cigarettes, bathroom-furniture, and cosmetics. Politicians have ruined words by a speech-easy usage, filling the same words with a different content than their opponents. The Nazis made some words have an evil ring, such as the 'showers' of Auschwitz. Fundamentally, we have seen such horrors in the twentieth century that what is the use of words?

Within literature itself, there are the problems caused by words becoming effete through over-use and by changing patterns of speech. As a modern German poet said:

> 'Fragments of everyday life, scraps of slang, words from the world of consumer goods force their way into the poetic text. The safety-pin and the Rapacki Plan, the juke-box and the cough-drop appear in verse with the same right and the same naturalness as the moon, the sea and the rose.'[10]

And all this says nothing of the inherent difficulties in using words, with their many-layered meanings and associations. The whole problem of language in modern literature forms one of the themes of the *Four Quartets*:

> '. . . That was a way of putting it—not very satisfactory:
> A periphrastic study in a worn-out poetical fashion,
> Leaving one still with the intolerable wrestle
> With words and meanings.'
> '. . . So here I am, in the middle way, having had twenty
>   years—
> Twenty years largely wasted, the years of *l'entre deux
>   guerres*—
> Trying to learn to use words, and every attempt
> Is a wholly new start, and a different kind of failure
> Because one has only learnt to get the better of words
> For the thing one no longer has to say, or the way in
>   which
> One is no longer disposed to say it. And so each venture
> Is a new beginning, a raid on the inarticulate
> With shabby equipment always deteriorating
> In the general mess of imprecision of feeling,
> Undisciplined squads of emotion.'
> '. . . The end is where we start from. And every phrase
> And sentence that is right (where every word is at home,
> Taking its place to support the others,
> The word neither diffident nor ostentatious,

> An easy commerce of the old and the new,
> The common word exact without vulgarity,
> The formal word precise but not pedantic,
> The complete consort dancing together)
> Every phrase and every sentence is an end and a
>   beginning,
> Every poem an epitaph.'[11]

A problem though words are, it is well for Kafka to remind us of their age-old power:

> 'It is entirely conceivable that life's splendour forever lies in wait about each one of us in all its fullness, but veiled from view, deep down, invisible, far off. It *is* there though, not hostile, not reluctant, not deaf. If you summon it by the right word, by its right name, it will come. This is the essence of magic, which does not create, but summons.'[12]

(c) *Symbolic Language*

'A symbol', wrote C. G. Jung, 'is a term, a name, or even a picture that may be familiar in daily life, yet that possesses specific connotations in addition to its conventional and obvious meaning. It implies something vague, unknown, or hidden from us. . . . It has a wider "unconscious" aspect that is never precisely defined or fully explained. Nor can one hope to define or explain it. As the mind explores the symbol, it is led to ideas that lie beyond the grasp of reason. . . . We constantly use symbolic terms to represent concepts that we cannot define or fully comprehend.'[13] Thus an artist uses symbols to enable him to mean more than he says.

The artist who uses symbols today, however, runs the risk of saying less than he means. This is especially true if his symbols are drawn from a mythological or religious context. With the breakdown of belief, such symbols have lost their force. The wheel, the cross, eagle, lion, ox, dove, mother and child, bread and wine have been thrown on Eliot's 'heap of broken images'. Even if unbroken, how wide an audience would understand allusions to biblical, Greek, let alone Norse mythology? And even if they did, how can mythologies possibly be awe-inspiring, and hence potent, when they are profoundly out-of-date and based on cosmologies well before Copernicus? There is a general sense of bric-à-brac.

Yet even if the symbols were still vivid, it has become more difficult for artists to use them. This is partly because modern man is conditioned by the thought-world of science, and prefers a literal and precise statement ('What is precise, cannot be true,' retorts Chagall), and partly because an artist is bound to use symbols self-consciously. He knows something of, and he knows that his audience knows something of, their psychological and anthropological significance. He feels inhibited.

The stream of symbols has either become shallow, or dried up. Of all this artists are more than aware:

'. . . We yearned for the swan-white tide, the divine affinity which unobtrusively permeates the differences of matter, of conditions, of events. . . .' (Arp)

'. . . But all is changed, that high horse riderless,
    Though mounted in that saddle Homer rode
    Where the swan drifts upon a darkening flood.' (Yeats)[14]

So language must be newly fashioned, and new symbols found. For the modern artist, this is likely to be not only a difficult search, but also a lonely one.

2. THE SEARCH

So the search was on, and still is, for a new art language, for new imaginative symbols. Artists search haphazardly, as the mood takes them—something remembered; an object found; a chance remark. All may be a starting point. For it is not a search for a finished product, but for a stimulus, a working idea for a creative mind.

'These masterful images because complete
    Grew in pure mind, but out of what began?'[15]

One way of beginning has been to raid the past. There has been a great interest in artists who handled problems like those of modern man, such as the threat from the darker side of human experience. Thus the bizarre and terrible imaginings of Bosch have been 'discovered', and belated praise given to Gotthelf's *The Black Spider*, where the creature, in a setting of idyllic rusticity,

becomes the menace of human evil. Artists have also returned to
just those periods and conventions which are in direct contrast
to the Victorians. Henry Moore, for instance, was more interested
in the harsh figures of archaic Greece, than in the harmonious
ones of fifth-century Athens. Similarly there has been an interest
in the metaphysical poets and dramatists of the early seventeenth
century ('Webster was much possessed by death . . .')—an epoch
close in its problems to our own. Again, there has been an interest
in the music of Bach because, rather than smooth-flowing harmonies, he has the built-in conflicts of counterpoint, as well as an
intellectual temper more congenial to modern man.

Another type of raid on the past has been for art-styles to
strengthen a national identity, such as the return of Bartók and
Kodaly to Hungarian folk music. As will be seen later, these are
not the only uses that artists make of the past: their common
feature has been an interest in earlier artists rather than in history
as such.

Artists have not only searched backward in time, but also outward into the world, to look at totally different art traditions and
conventions. One such interest was unavoidable: American jazz
music. It is reflected in such works as Stravinsky's *Histoire d'un
Soldat*, and Milhaud's *La Création du Monde*. Others were more
individual, such as Braque's in Negro art:

> '. . . opened up for me a new horizon. It permitted me to
> make contact with instinctive things, with direct manifestations
> which were in direct opposition to the false traditionalism
> which I abhorred. . . .'[16]

Other artists were to follow him in this interest in the primitive—
a theme returned to in the chapter 'The World Dialogue'.

From the world without to the world within themselves. 'My
"engagement" ', wrote Cocteau, 'is to lose myself in the ultimate,
most uncomfortable depths of my being. . . . It is from our re-
serves, from our night that things come to us. Our works pre-
exist within us. The problem is to discover it. We are merely its
archaeologists.'[17] A metaphor of the search is also used by the
Japanese novelist, Yukio Mishima:

> '. . . Writing is digging, digging, digging, and hoping that
> one will sometime reach the springs. My room is like Proust's,

one covered with cork. It is my prison but through it I reach
my freedom.'[18]

Sometimes one meets the idea of inspiration—not fashionable
today. Hindemith, for instance, speaks of the 'region of visionary
irrationality in which the veiled secrets of art dwell', which he
cannot enter: 'he can only pray to be elected one of its messen-
gers'.[19]

Some artists, however, stimulated by Freud, tried deliberately
to exploit the irrational. This was the aim of Breton and the
Surrealists. Max Ernst realized their force:

> 'The association of a sewing machine and an umbrella on a
> surgical table is a familiar example . . . of the phenomenon dis-
> covered by the surrealists, that the association of two (or more)
> apparently alien elements on a plane alien to both is the most
> potent ignition of poetry.'[20]

Ernst, himself well-read in psychology, realized that a self-
conscious knowledge of symbols could cramp his work. To overcome this he played with the trick of *frottage*. As he said:

> 'In order to give foundation to my powers of meditation and
> hallucination, I made a series of drawings of the tiles by laying
> sheets of paper on them at random and then taking graphite
> rubbings. When I fixed my eyes on the result, I was astounded
> by a suddenly sharpened sense of a hallucinatory series of con-
> trasting and superimposed pictures.'[20]

He claimed that *frottage* 'by enlarging the active part of the mind's
hallucinatory faculties'[20] enabled him to attend, simply as a spectator, the birth of his works.

As well as exploring their own inner world, artists explored, as
they always have, the immediate world of their own lives and
surroundings, with, as Henry James claimed, 'an immense sensibility, a kind of huge spider-web, of the finest silken threads,
suspended in the chamber of consciousness and catching every
air-borne particle in its tissue'.[21] Sometimes this has meant the
'rediscovery of a primary impetus, the elementary principle of all
art, in the local conditions'.[22] Visual artists have developed the
sharpest alertness for material objects, not least isolated and

neglected ones '. . . to collect things washed up by the tide. Things lying there, waiting for someone to discover their personality.'[23]

Not only painters, however, have been fascinated by the material world. The Chilean poet, Pablo Neruda, has the same sympathy for inanimate things:

'It is very appropriate at certain times of day or night, to look deeply into objects at rest: wheels which have traversed vast dusty spaces, bearing great cargoes of vegetables or minerals, sacks from the coal-yards, barrels, baskets, the handles and grips of the carpenter's tools. They exude the touch of man and the earth as a lesson to the tormented poet. Worn surfaces, the mark hands have left on things, the aura, sometimes tragic and always wistful, of these objects, lend to reality a fascination not to be taken lightly.

'The flawed confusion of human beings shows in them, the proliferating materials used and discarded, the prints of feet and fingers, the permanent mark of humanity on the inside and outside of all objects.

'That is the kind of poetry we should be after, poetry worn away as if by acid, by the labour of hands, impregnated with sweat and smoke, smelling of lilies and of urine, splashed by the variety of what we do, legally or illegally.

'A poetry as impure as old clothes, as a body with its food-stains and its shame, with wrinkles, observations, dreams, wakefulness, prophecies, declarations of love and hate, stupid-ities, shocks, idylls, political beliefs, negations, doubts, affirma-tions, taxes.'[24]

Not unlike Yeats, Neruda found the need to

'. . . lie down where all the ladders start,
In the foul rag-and-bone shop of the heart.'[25]

Wherever the search of modern artists has been—in the art forms of earlier ages, in the world, in their own depths, in the experience of their senses—the common ground has been a con-cern for the present. As Franz Marc said:

'The great artists do not seek their forms in the mist of the past, but take the deepest soundings they can of the genuine, profoundest centre of gravity of their age.'[26]

3. THE MAKING

An artist is not just a curio hunter. Such an apparently desultory hunting in time, the world, the inner self, and the senses could produce nothing but a rag-bag of styles and a jumble of impressions; or it might make an artist too vulnerable to the irrational, or too self-conscious, or make his work too private and esoteric, and so convey nothing to his audience. So far then the search need not have produced more than jottings or sketches, and there need have been no emergence of new forms. How then do 'these masterful images become complete' and 'grow in pure mind', from wherever they began?

The simple answer is that nobody knows. Artists, however, seem ready to try to explain. So Picasso:

'A picture is not thought out and settled beforehand. While it is being done it changes as one's thoughts change. And when it is finished, it still goes on changing, according to the state of mind of whoever is looking at it. . . When you begin a picture, you often make some pretty discoveries. You must be on guard against these. Destroy the thing, do it over several times. In each destroying of a beautiful discovery, the artist does not really suppress it, but rather transforms it, condenses it, makes it more substantial. What comes out in the end is the result of discarded finds. Otherwise, you become your own connoisseur. I sell myself nothing.'[55]

The public, however, may think that he has sold their idea of an artist, for it runs counter to two popular beliefs of artistic creation. One is the idea of the artist as an inspired being, through whom the the Spirit pours. His function is to be passive; and the result is to be admired, not exposed to reflection and response. The other is that the artist has some deep, emotional experience, and only then calls his technical skill into play to express it. Against these ideas, artists would not only want to emphasize their own activity, but also that technical excitement, curiosity, and experiment are continuous from start to finish. It seems better for the artists to speak for themselves.

(i) *Two Painters*

Paul Klee: '. . . While the artist is still exerting all his efforts to group the formal elements purely and logically so that each in its place is right and none clashes with the other, a layman, watching from behind, pronounces the devastating words "But that isn't a bit like uncle". The artist, if his nerve is disciplined, thinks to himself, "To hell with uncle! I must get on with my building. . . . This new brick is a little too heavy and to my mind puts too much weight on the left; I must add a good-sized counterweight on the right to restore the equilibrium."

'And he adds to this side and that until finally the scales show a balance.

'And he is relieved if, in the end, the shaking which he has perforce had to give his original pure structure of good elements, has only gone so far as to provide that opposition which exists as contrast in a living picture.

'But, sooner or later, the association of ideas may of itself occur to him, without the intervention of a layman. Nothing need then prevent him from accepting it, provided that it introduces itself under its proper title.

'Acceptance of this material association may suggest additions which, once the subject is formulated, clearly stand in essential relationship to it. If the artist is fortunate, these natural forms may fit into a slight gap in the formal composition, as though they had always belonged there.'[28]

*

Georges Braque: 'No object can be tied down to any one sort of reality; a stone may be part of a wall, a lethal weapon, a pebble on a beach, or anything else you like, just as this file in my hand can be metamorphosed into a shoe-horn or a spoon, according to the way in which I use it. The first time this phenomenon struck me was in the trenches during the First World War when my batman turned a bucket into a brazier by poking a few holes into it with his bayonet and filling it with coke. For me this commonplace incident had a poetic significance: I began to see things in a new way. Everything, I realized, is subject to metamorphosis; everything changes according to circumstances. So when you ask me whether a particular form in one of my paintings depicts a woman's head, a fish, a vase, or all four at once, I can't give you a categorical answer, for this "metamorphic" confusion is fundamental to what I am out to express. It's all the same to me whether a form represents a different thing to different people or many things at the same time. And then I occasionally introduce forms which have no literal meaning whatsoever. Sometimes these are accidents which happen to suit my purpose, sometimes "rhymes" which echo other forms, and sometimes rhythmical motifs which help to integrate a composition and give it movement.'[29]

(ii) *A Poet*

Pasternak: 'After two or three stanzas and several images by which he was himself astonished, his work took possession of him and he experienced the approach of what is called inspiration. At such moments the correlation of the forces controlling the artist is, as it were, stood on its head. The ascendancy is no longer with the artist or the state of mind which he is trying to express, but with language, his instrument of expression. Language, the home and dwelling of meaning and beauty, itself begins to think and speak for man and turns wholly into music, not in the sense of outward, audible sounds but by virtue of the power and momentum of its inward flow. Then, like the current of a mighty river polishing stones and turning wheels by its very movement, the flow of speech creates in passing, by the force of its own laws, rhyme and rhythm and countless other forms and formations, still more important and until now undiscovered, unconsidered and unnamed.

'At such moments Yuri felt that the main part of his work was not being done by him but by something which was above him and controlling him: the thought and poetry of the world as it was at that moment and as it would be in the future. He was controlled by the next step it was to take in the order of its historical development; and he felt himself to be only the pretext and the pivot setting it in motion.

'This feeling relieved him for a time of self-reproach, of dissatisfaction with himself, of the sense of his own nothingness.'[30]

(iii) *A Musician*

Stravinsky: '. . . I maintain that inspiration is in no way a prescribed condition of the creative act, but rather a manifestation that is chronologically secondary. . . . Step by step, link by link, it will be granted to (the composer) to discover the whole. It is this chain of discoveries, as well as each individual discovery, that give rise to the emotion—an almost physiological reflex, like that of appetite causing a flow of saliva—this emotion which invariably follows closely the phases of the creative process. . . . All creation presupposes at its origin a sort of appetite that is brought on by the foretaste of discovery.

'. . . The faculty of creating is never given to us all by itself. It always goes hand in hand with the gift of observation. And the true creator may be recognized by his ability always to find about him, in the commonest and humblest thing, items worthy of note. . . . The least accident holds his interest and guides his operations. . . . One does not contrive an accident; one observes it to draw inspiration therefrom. An accident is perhaps the only thing that really inspires us. A composer improvises aimlessly the way an animal grubs about. . . . So we grub about in expectation of our pleasure, guided by our scent, and suddenly we stumble against an unknown obstacle. It gives us a jolt, a shock, and this shock fecundates our creative power. . . .

'. . . The creator's function is to sift the elements he receives from (the imagination), for human activity must impose limits upon itself. The more art is controlled, limited, worked over, the more it is free.'[31]

(iv) *A Film Director*

Eisenstein: 'In the work period the basic selection is transmuted, not into logical evaluation, as in a post-analysis . . . but into direct action. . . . The artist thinks directly in terms of manipulating his resources and materials. His thoughts are transmuted into direct action, formulated not by a formula, but by a form. . . .

'Turning to the creative process, we shall see that it proceeds in the following manner. Before the inner vision, before the perception of the creator, hovers a given image, emotionally embodying his theme. The task that confronts him is to transform this image into a few basic partial representations which, in their combination and juxtaposition, shall evoke in the consciousness and feelings of the spectator, reader, or auditor, that same initial general image which originally hovered before the creative artist. . . .

'. . . The image planned by the author has become flesh of the spectator's risen image. . . . Within me, as a spectator, this image is born and grown. Not only the author has created, but I also —the creating spectator—have participated.'[32]

*

One has returned to Picasso's insistence that the creative process goes on after the artist himself has finished—'changing, according to the state of mind of whoever is looking at it'.

Yet reading these comments by modern artists may still give rise to a doubt: they are too self-conscious. An artist's work, it may be suggested, can only be cramped by such rationalizing. One answer would be to appreciate the danger, but to insist that in a period of the breakdown of values and conventions, the only way forward is an extreme self-awareness of what one is trying to do and why, just as mental health may only come through greater consciousness.

Another answer is hinted at by comparing two statements:

'There must be, in every canvas, a precise point, a given moment—"a fly's eye"—where everything tilts, where the call of the wild intersects the call of duty. . . . On a huge canvas. A simple line and a red circle as final period. But how that period is placed! With infinitesimal precision. You can't move it by a hair's breadth. Yes, I have done things like that in the past, but I relied on sensitiveness. They were like the respiration of life.' (Joan Miró)[33]

'Last summer I walked in a field near Avebury where two rough monoliths stand up, sixteen feet high, miraculously patterned with black and orange lichen, remnants of an avenue of stones which led to the Great Circle. A mile away, a green pyramid casts a gigantic shadow. In the hedge, at hand, the white trumpet of a convolvulus turns from its spiral stem, following the sun. In my art I would solve such an equation.' (Paul Nash)[34]

There is no basic conflict here on what painting is about, but patently there are two different personalities, approaching their work in somewhat contrasting ways, and using intuition and rational thought to a different degree. One could press it further and suggest that here is something of the divide that has been continuous in the history of art: 'Abstraction and Empathy', classical and romantic, the 'constructive' and the 'organic', Apollo and Dionysus. The outstanding feature of modern art is not that, taken as a whole, it is more intellectual, but that the widest extremes exist side by side: the most highly cerebral and the most visceral. The real doubt is whether, in such a situation of diversity, the language of any art can serve its main purpose of communication.

4. THE FINDING

In their searches and work, modern artists have been trying to establish new languages. Have they been successful? How far a new symbolic language has emerged will be touched on more fully in the second half of this section. The question for the moment is how far artists have developed successful working languages within their own media.

Certainly it would be easy to find examples of such language-making. One outstanding language-maker in music, for example, has been Schoenberg. He realized that he must do more than satisfy his own senses. The artist, he said:

'. . . will wish to know *consciously* the laws and rules which govern the forms which he has conceived "as in a dream". Strongly convincing as this dream may have been, the conviction that these new sounds obey the laws of nature and of our manner of thinking—the conviction that order, logic, comprehensibility and form cannot be present without obedience to such laws—forces the composer along the road of exploration. He must find, if not laws or rules, at least ways to justify the dissonant character of these harmonies and their successions.

'After many unsuccessful attempts during a period of approximately twelve years, I laid the foundations for a new procedure in musical construction which seemed fitted to replace those structural differentiations provided formerly by tonal harmonies.

'I called this procedure *Method of Composing with Twelve Tones Which Are Related Only With One Another*.

'This method consists primarily of the constant and exclusive use of a set of twelve different tones. This means, of course, that no tone is repeated within the series and that it uses all twelve tones of the chromatic scale, though in a different order. . . .'[35]

Schoenberg realized that such a new language offered no

easy alternative to the harmonies of the romantics, but would throw a composer back onto his own resources:

'The introduction of my method of composing with twelve tones does not facilitate composing. . . . The restrictions imposed are so severe that they can only be overcome by an imagination which has survived a tremendous number of adventures.'[35]

Such an imagination was that of James Joyce. Equipped with a sharp musical ear and a knowledge of European languages, he explored the possibilities of verbal language:

'*brings us to* Howth Castle & Environs! Sir Tristram, *viola d'amores*, had **passencore rearrived** *on a merry isthmus* from North Armorica *to wielderfight his peninsular war*, nor **sham rocks** *by the Oconee* **exaggerated themselse to** Laurens county, Ga, doubling all the time, nor a voice **from afire bellowsed** mishe **chishe** to tufftuff **thouartpeatrick** —.' (Opening sentence of 1926 version of *Finnegans Wake*.)[36]

Finnegans Wake was not published till 1939, and represents about sixteen years of persistent thought and revision, and many passages are far more dense and difficult than these opening words. The bald question is inevitable: has Joyce pressed language beyond the limits of understanding? At the very least, are the demands made of the reader too great?

Two arts which seem more public and more naturally a part of the twentieth century—architecture and the cinema—also experienced the need to struggle with language-making. In the cinema, the need was to develop a language of its own, as distinct from being a photograph of a play. One finds Eisenstein, for instance, exploring montage—'two film pieces of any kind placed together, inevitably combine into a new concept, arising out of that juxtaposition'—and with the 'question of finding an inner synchronization between the tangible picture and the differently perceived sounds'.[37] The architect's language was formed by rejecting the aesthetics of *The Stones of Venice*, and interknitting two elements: contemporary technical possibilities and the demands of social function. As Frank Lloyd Wright tried to explain:

'Organic architecture is an architecture from within outward, in which entity is the ideal. . . . Organic means intrinsic—in the

philosophic sense, entity—wherever the whole is to the part
as the part is to the whole and where the nature of the materials,
the nature of the purpose, the nature of the entire performance
becomes clear as a necessity. Out of that nature comes what
character in any particular situation you can give to the building
as a creative artist. . . .

'. . . Something had to be done with these new materials—
these great new resources—glass and steel and the machine.
They are tremendous. Because of that principle of tenuity in
steel we could use the cantilever, and into structure by way of
steel came this element of continuity. You can see one thing
merging into another and being of another rather than this old
cut, butt, and slash.'[38]

Corbusier added to such thinking the need to develop a set of
working standards to achieve such purposes, which he called his
Modulor: 'A Harmonious Measure to the Human Scale Universally Applicable to Architecture and Mechanics.'[39]

The visual arts probably provide more examples of language-
making than any other, from Cubism and Surrealism to 'Abstract
Expressionism, Post Painterly Abstraction, Hard Edge and "Situation", English Pop, American Neo-Dada, American Pop, and
Kinetic Art,' to quote from a recent list. Such proliferation only
forces one back to some of the questions already implied: are
these new languages—in whatever medium—anything more than
an isolated personal discovery, valid for that artist alone? Or can
they be shared and developed by fellow artists, and have more
permanency than a group popularity? Can they also convey meaning to a wider audience than the initiates?

It is hoped that the second part of this section will provide some
such test of their validity as true languages.

★

This chapter has been preoccupied with the working problems
of the artist. It has tried to show the other side of the dialogue to
the demands of society on the artist. It began by suggesting that
artists create out of their own distress; it remains to ask why then
their work matters to anybody else. Their answers will form a
useful introduction to the rest of the book, which explores artists'
experience of the modern world:

'What every poet starts from is his own emotions. . . . Shakespeare, too, was occupied with the struggle—which alone constitutes life for a poet—to transmute his personal and private agonies into something rich and strange, something universal and impersonal.' (T. S. Eliot)[40]

'All art is a revolt against man's fate.' (Malraux)[41]

'What do you think an artist is? An imbecile who has only his eyes if he is a painter, or ears if he is a musician? On the contrary, he is at the same time a political being, constantly alive to heart-rending, fiery or happy events, to which he responds in every way. How would it be possible to feel no interest in other people . . . to detach yourself from the life they so copiously bring you? No, painting is not done to decorate apartments. It is an instrument . . . for attack and defence against the enemy.' (Picasso)[42]

'Because a work does not aim at reproducing natural appearances it is not, therefore, an escape from life but it may be a penetration into reality, not a sedative or drug, not the exercise of good taste, the provision of pleasant shapes and colours in a pleasing combination, not a decoration to life, but an expression of the significance of life, a stimulation to greater effort of living.' (Henry Moore)[43]

'The work is an expression of a certain attitude; the attitude takes shape, that is, becomes organized and is a living organism containing within itself all the antagonisms which must enter into its make-up without destroying it. The more complex and numerous the contrasts, the tensions, the passions, the more important the work, and since the work is like a living organism, like a being or an entity, by the same token it is invention and discovery, imaginary and real, useful and useless, necessary and superfluous, objective and subjective, literature and truth. It is the outcome of play-activity which is free from falsehood. Of course, you may reject the work or consider it harmful, just as you may condemn or kill a human being.' (Ionesco)[44]

REFERENCES

1. MONTHERLANT, H. DE: *The Lepers* (New York: Musson, 1940). KAFKA, F.: Quoted from TIPPETT, M.: *Moving into Aquarius* (Routledge, 1959), p. 109. The full context is given—'the poet is much smaller and weaker than the average man of society'—in an essay where Tippett explores the difference between the modern world and that of Mozart. VAN GOGH, V.: *The Complete Letters of Vincent Van Gogh* (3 vols., Thames and Hudson, 1958).* From letter 531, Vol. 3, p. 25. A valuable study of Van Gogh is GRAETZ, H. R.: *The Symbolic Language of Vincent Van Gogh* (Thames and Hudson, 1963), where this remark is quoted.*

2. STRAVINSKY, I.: From VLAD, ROMAN: *Stravinsky*, tr. by F. and A. Fuller (O.U.P., 1960), p. 113. From a statement by Stravinsky at the first performance of his 'melodrama' *Persephone*, in 1934.*

3. MOORE, H.: *Henry Moore on Sculpture*—a collection of the sculptor's writings and spoken works, edited with an introduction by Philip James (Macdonald, 1966).* From the article 'Unit One', p. 72. ('Unit One' first appeared in a book of that title, edited by Herbert Read, Cassell, 1934).

4. MIRÓ, J.: Quoted from SCHNEIDER, P.: 'At the Louvre with Miró', *Encounter*, March 1956, Vol. XXIV, No. 3, p. 44.

5. ELIOT, T. S.: From his introduction to JONES, D.: *In Parenthesis* (Faber, 1937. Also paperback).*

6. BRAQUE, G.: Quoted from RICHARDSON, J.: *Braque* (Penguin Modern Painters), Introduction.

7. YEATS, W. B.: WADE, A. (ed.): *The Letters of W. B. Yeats* (Hart-Davis, 1954).*

8. COCTEAU, J., and FRAIGNEAU, A.: op. cit., p. 23.

9. STRAVINSKY, I.: *Poetics of Music*, op. cit., p. 51.

10. ENZENSBERGER, H. M.: 'In Search of the Lost Language', *Encounter*, September 1963, Vol. XXI, No. 3, p. 49.

11. ELIOT, T. S.: *Four Quartets*, op. cit. From 'East Coker' and 'Little Gidding'.

12. KAFKA, F.: *The Diaries of Franz Kafka* (1914–1923). Ed. by Max Brod (Secker, 1949).* Entry for October 18, 1921, p. 195. See the delightful article by Idris Parry: 'Kafka, Rilke and Rumpelstiltskin' (*Listener*, December 2, 1965).

13. JUNG, C. G.: op. cit., Part I; *Approaching the Unconscious*, pp. 20–1.

14. ARP, H.: Quoted from David Sylvester's article 'Art as Conspiracy' (*New Statesman*, September 22, 1961).

YEATS, W. B.: *Selected Poems*, op. cit. From the poem 'Coole Park and Ballylee, 1931'.

15. YEATS, W. B.: *Selected Poems*, op. cit. From the poem 'The Circus Animals' Desertion', part III.

16. BRAQUE, G.: Quoted from RICHARDSON, op. cit., Introduction.

17. COCTEAU., J., and FRAIGNEAU, A.: op. cit., pp. 58, 131.

18. MISHIMA, Y.: From an interview reported in *The Guardian*. Available works include: *After the Banquet* (Secker 1957)* and *Temple of the Golden Pavilion* (Secker, 1959).*

19. HINDEMITH, P.: *A Composer's World* (O.U.P., 1952) p. 221.

20. ERNST, M.: Quoted from JUNG, C. G. op. cit. Part 4: Symbolism in the Visual Arts' by Aniela Jaffé, pp. 258–9. See Max Ernst's book, *Beyond Painting* (New York, 1948).

21. JAMES, H.: *The House of Fiction* (Rupert Hart-Davis, 1957). From the essay 'The Art of Fiction', p. 31.

22. WILLIAMS, W. C. Quoted from Moore, G. (ed.): *The Penguin Book of Modern American Verse*, p. 86.

23. MIRÓ, J.: Quoted from JUNG, C. G., op. cit. (Aniela Jaffé), p. 253.

24. NERUDA, P.: *On Impure Poetry*. Quoted from REID. A.: 'A Visit to Neruda', *Encounter*, September, 1965, Vol. XXV, No. 3, pp. 67–8.

25. YEATS. W. B.: See note (15) in this section.

26. MARC, F.: Quoted from JUNG, C. G., op. cit. (Aniela Jaffé), p. 250.

27. PICASSO, P.: Quoted from WILSON, J. (ed.): *The Faith of an Artist*, op. cit., p. 179. (Original source—BARR, A. H., Jr.: *Picasso: Fifty Years of His Art*. New York, Museum of Modern Art, 1939).

28. KLEE, P.: *On Modern Art*. Easiest available translation is published as a Faber paperback, 1966, with an introduction by Herbert Read. This passage was translated by E. H. Gombrich—see (30) below.

29. BRAQUE, G.: Quoted from RICHARDSON, op. cit., Introduction.

30. PASTERNAK, B.: *Doctor Zhivago*. Tr. M. Hayward and M. Harari (Collins & Harvill, 1958), pp. 391–2.* The passages from Klee (28) and Pasternak are quoted and discussed by GOMBRICH, E. H.: 'Freud's Aesthetics', in *Encounter*, January 1966, Vol. XXVI, No. 1, pp. 36–8.

31. STRAVINSKY, I.: *Poetics of Music*, op. cit., pp. 50–1, 54, 56, 36.

32. EISENSTEIN, S. M.: *The Film Sense* (Faber, 1943), pp. 33, 36.*

33. MIRÓ, J.: Quoted from SCHNEIDER, op. cit., pp. 43–4.

34. NASH, P.: Quoted from READ, H.: *Paul Nash* (Penguin Modern Painters), Introduction.

35. SCHOENBERG, A.: *Style and Idea*, op. cit., pp. 106–7.

36. JOYCE, J.: *A First-Draft Version of Finnegans Wake*. Edited and annotated by D. Hayman (Faber, 1963).* Joyce's additions are in italics, his substitutions in bold face. It is interesting to com-

pare the opening sentence of the final version of *Finnegans Wake* (Faber, 1939)*—'riverun, past Eve and Adam's, from swerve of shore to bend of bay, brings us by a commodius vicus of recirculation back to Howth Castle and Environs.'

37. EISENSTEIN, S.: *The Film Sense*, op. cit., p. 14.
38. WRIGHT, F. LLOYD.: *The Future of Architecture* (Architectural Press, London, 1955), pp. 13, 21.*
39. LE CORBUSIER.: *The Modulor* (Faber, 1954. Also paperback).*
40. ELIOT, T. S.: *Selected Essays* (Faber, 1951). From the essay 'Shakespeare and the Stoicism of Seneca', p. 137.*
41. MALRAUX, A.: *The Voices of Silence*, op. cit., p. 639.
42. PICASSO, P.: From BARR, A. H., Jr.: *Picasso: Fifty Years of His Art* (Museum of Modern Art, 1946), pp. 247–8. From a written statement by Picasso himself in the spring of 1945, soon after he had declared himself a communist. About this time he was painting *The Charnel House*.
43. MOORE, H.: *Henry Moore on Sculpture*, op. cit., 'Unit One', p. 72.
44. IONESCO, E.: 'The Writer and his Problems'. From *Encounter*, September 1964, Vol. XXIII, No. 3, p. 10. Tr. by John Weightman.

PART TWO

THE SEARCH
EXPLORING CONTEMPORARY REALITY

CHAPTER ONE

The Threatened Individual

'NATURE might stand up, and say to all the world, "This was a man!" ' Such confidence in the individual human being had a long life and was backed by the growth of political and economic liberalism. In the arts, it gave confidence to the portrait painter, the novelist, the lyric poet: 'I am the master of my fate: I am the captain of my soul!' But the jig was up. As suggested at the start, Freud and Marx, mass urban living, and the death of millions in war set so deep a doubt in men's minds, that they had to start thinking again.

I. INTROSPECTION: 'WHO AM I?'

Detailed knowledge of an individual in modern society is likely to be in the form of either a case-history or a dossier, a record of illness or of crime. And when the individual comes to explore himself he is likely to become aware of both elements, the anti-social and the neurotic. For in following the Greek advice of 'Know Thyself', modern man is predisposed to see the dark side of himself. Jung called this the Shadow—a term used by Eliot and giving force to his words:

> 'Between the idea
> And the reality
> Between the motion
> And the act
> Falls the Shadow. . . .'[1]

They come from the poem 'The Hollow Men', which was itself prefaced with a quotation from Conrad's 'shadow' study, *The*

Heart of Darkness. If modern man, however, gave a different picture of 'himself', so also has he given a different meaning to 'knowing'. 'Knowing' must be scalpel-sharp, an X-ray probe, ruthless,
scientific. He wanted, as it were, to give himself up to the full
rigour of a Freudian analysis, and to do it in public. To be, as the
Marquis de Sade wishes at the end of Peter Weiss's *Marat*,
'utterly naked, utterly aware'.[2]

If the nude and the portrait seemed lost to the camera, painting
was still capable of indecent exposures—'indecent' in the sense
that the artist had stripped away all ornamental and polite conventions. The portraits, for instance, of Kokoschka, Wyndham
Lewis, Sutherland and Picasso have a ruthless observation, giving
a sense, not of admiration, but of revelation. Even more disturbing are the characters of Francis Bacon, not individuals so
much as types—a pope, a business man, a lover—that could be
any one of us. Here is paint, to use Bacon's own distinction, 'which
comes across directly on the nervous system' rather than paint
which 'tells you the story in a long diatribe through the brain.'
'Man', said Bacon, 'is haunted by the mystery of his existence and
is therefore much more obsessed with the making and recording
of his own image on his world than with the beautiful fun of even
the best abstract art. . . . Art unlocks the valves of intuition
and perception about the human situation at a deeper level.' To
suggest a meaning to such pictures would be wrong; not just because, as he insists, the meaning is in the paint, but also because
they carry with them that dark aura, whose waves disturb the
onlooker, and each one differently. 'Art is a method of opening up
areas of feeling rather than merely an illustration of an object.'[3]

In Bacon's figures there exists a sense of undiscovered evil,
and so much of literature from *Crime and Punishment* through
the detective story to the 'Theatre of Cruelty' is the search to find
out the guilty, or, when known, to probe the mind of the mur-
derer. It may be to avoid being overwhelmed in the search that
artists have found it valuable to use the patterns of Greek myth,
not least of the blood-stained House of Atreus: Agamemnon slain
by his wife's lover; she in revenge slain by her son, Orestes, in-
cited by his sister, Elektra; Orestes driven out by the Eumenides.
Elektra comes in an opera by Strauss and plays by Giraudoux
and Eugene O'Neill. The situation was also used by Sartre in
The Flies and Eliot in *The Family Reunion*. Leaving aside the

luckless Oedipus, given prestige treatment in Freud, Greek myth has also returned in the minotaurs, fauns, and satyrs of Picasso, bringing both menace and a mercurial gaiety with them.

Satyrs are a reminder of an irrational 'hectic in the blood', the animal side of man, another part of the repressed darkness. But where can such things live today? Man senses a division: his ultra-modern mind keeps company with archaic creatures. It is a division which has sometimes been focused in polarity of masculinity and femininity—a tension which some artists have felt in their own lives. It has been suggested for instance that one reason for Lawrence's preoccupation with the sex act was his own need of a fusion of these two elements within himself. Such a problem is hinted at in the development of his own writing. In an early book, *Sons and Lovers*, he explores himself in more or less direct autobiography, whereas in *The Rainbow* and *Women in Love* the focus of his search has switched to Ursula, a possible expression of his inner feminine side. She stands in close relation to, but is separate from Birkin, who outwardly is a self-portrait of Lawrence himself. Martin Esslin in his book *Brecht: A Choice of Evils*, in a closely argued and documented chapter ('Reason Versus Instinct'), shows a similar conflict in Brecht, neatly articulated in his play *The Good Woman of Setzuan*. Here the central character is at one and the same time a compassionate woman, who saves the young airman from suicide, and a ruthless man, the Capitalist, who exploits the workers in the tobacco factory. It is a tension which appears throughout Brecht, in the pull between his reason —the Communist and dramatic theorist—on the one hand, and the instinctive poet on the other.

> 'I am the most practical of all my brethren—
> And *my* head comes first of all!
> My brethren were cruel, I am the cruellest—
> And *I* weep in the night!'[4]

If tears and thoughts, masculinity and femininity, make modern man divided, this may force some artists to explore, not just the myths, but the archetypes which lie deeper than the personal problem of the artist himself. An outstanding explorer of this elemental world is Henry Moore. 'There are', said Moore, 'two particular motives or subjects which I have constantly used in my sculpture in the last twenty years: they are the "Reclining

Figure" idea and the "Mother and Child" idea. Perhaps of the two the "Mother and Child" has been the more fundamental obsession.'[5] The psychologist Erich Neumann has explored Moore's work in his illuminating study *The Archetypal World of Henry Moore*:

> 'The emergence of an archetype, i.e. a collective unconscious content active in the psyche of large numbers of people, makes itself felt in many fields. Its coming to consciousness finds expression in psychic disturbances as well as in the creative processes of art, in sociological changes as well as in the revaluations of philosophy. One of the central problems of our age is the activation of the earth archetype, and more particularly of the feminine archetype in general.'[6]

Such an activation—in both its hostile and healing aspects—has been central to Moore's work.

Solid rock figures, however, are the last thing that some artists would use as a symbol of modern man, for they doubt his very reality, in particular the identity of the individual. A small but continuous undercurrent of works questions the conscious 'I': Pirandello's *Six Characters in Search of an Author*, for instance, or more recently, Max Frisch's *I'm Not Stiller*. One of the frightening features of Kafka's novels is that the doomed central figure is never more than an anonymous initial, K. Even more striking are the wide areas of modern painting where no human form ever smudges the deserts of abstraction.

If this is man in the twentieth century—dark, divided, disturbed, and doubtful of his own identity—how can such a creature ever act effectively? How can he ever decide, relate to others, or make some heroic mark on his world?

2. 'LOSE THE NAME OF ACTION'

The problem of action was Hamlet's, and modern man shares his hesitancy and doubts, even his contemplation of suicide. Two oft-asked questions underline real difficulties. 'What can *I* do about it?'—meaning that any action taken by an individual will not affect the situation at all, because it is too vast. 'Whatever shall I *do*?'—meaning that some action is unavoidable, but that it is difficult to know what to do for the best. Predecessors may have had a more helpful framework in which to decide.

One answer, of course, is to hang on to that framework. A powerful symbol here is the theme of Hermann Broch's great novel, *The Sleepwalkers*.[7] Men act, it is suggested, out of habitual responses, without being awake to, or adapting to, the changing reality of the world. The novel, in three parts, stretches across the Kaiser's Germany: *The Romantic* (1888); *The Anarchist* (1902); *The Realist* (1918). None of these rôles is a sufficient coming-to-terms with the crisis in European values—a discussion of this crisis intersperses the narrative chapters. It is the aristocratic class, personified in the rigid and gracious Joachim von Pasenow, which is the least successful. The theme is handled again in such books as Thomas Mann's *Buddenbrooks*, Lampedusa's *The Leopard*, and even in *Dr. Zhivago*. Whether treated with pathos or humour, or as an analysis of decay, the theme is that European values, as a guide to action, are 'no longer wholly in the present'.

If men caught in a decaying tradition cannot act effectively, neither it seems can the puny individual in modern mass society. The complement to *The Sleepwalkers* is *The Insect Play*, in which man is as insignificant as the ants, or another play of Capek's, *R.U.R.*, in which man is crushed by robots. The theme is taken up in Ernst Toller's *Masses and Men*, and also by another figure of German expressionism (and extreme political opinion), Bertolt Brecht in *Man Equals Man*:

'. . . Mr. Bertolt Brecht will prove that one can
Do whatever one wants to do with a man:
A man will be reassembled like a motor-car tonight in front
   of you—
And afterwards will be as good as new. . . .'[8]

A man was to be taken to bits, not to reveal his nature, as much as to show that society determined his attitudes and actions. The diagnosis was taken up in Huxley's *Brave New World* and Orwell's *1984*. One of the most depressing symbols here is that of Ilse Aichinger's *The Bound Man*:

'. . . his legs were tied all the way up to his thighs; a single length of rope was tied round his ankles, criss-crossed all the way up his legs, and encircled his hips, his chest and his arms. He could not see where it was knotted. He showed no sign of fear or hurry, though he thought he was unable to move, until he discovered that the rope allowed his legs some free play too. This made him smile, and it occurred to him that perhaps children had been playing a practical joke on him. . . .'

But stay there he does, and becomes exploited as a circus-clown. '. . . The freedom that he enjoyed in this struggle was having to adapt every movement of his limbs to the rope that tied him. . . .'[9]

Even the bound man, then, has some freedom of movement. And some modern writers explore, so to speak, the slack on the rope. One such explored theme is that of conscience, when the individual is in conflict with society. This has been handled by writers from within a Christian orthodoxy, such as the Catholic novelist, Werner Bergengruen. In his novel *Der Grosstyrann und das Gericht* (published in the U.K. as *A Matter of Conscience*) the problem is what to do when the wrong-doer is the ruler himself. 'This book', runs the preamble, 'tells of the temptations that beset the mighty and of the corruptibility of the unmighty and the threatened. It tells of divers happenings in the town of Cassano, of the slaying of one and the guilt of all men. . . .'[10] Although the setting is Renaissance Italy, Bergengruen was writing both within and about Hitler's Germany.

Another German handling of this issue is in Brecht's *Galileo*, though here the essential context is the scientific search for the atomic bomb. The turning point of the play is when Galileo, for all the mental toughness of his search for truth, breaks down at the mere sight of the instruments of torture. When an admiring disciple visits him in prison, he frankly admits: '. . . I surrendered my knowledge to those in power, to use, or not to use, or to misuse, just as suited their purposes. I have betrayed my profession. A man who does what I have done cannot be tolerated in the ranks of science.'[11] And he turns to guzzle a goose.

From a goose to the starved life below decks in the British Navy during the Napoleonic Wars: namely, Benjamin Britten's opera *Billy Budd*, based on Herman Melville's story. In the background is Britten's own conflict with the state as a conscientious objector in the Second World War. The immediate problem before Captain Vere, in the opera, is whether he should or should not order that Budd be hanged. Clearly he has murdered Taggart, a superior officer; and equally clearly, in His Majesty's Regulations, the punishment is death. Yet it is equally true that Taggart was a sadistic bully, who misused his powers as an officer, and that he had provoked Billy Budd by mocking his stammer. Captain Vere knew the whole story and was a humane and fair-minded man. Nevertheless Budd hangs.

Law and the state had won. The possibility of the individual's defiance of the state is taken up by Anouilh in *Antigone*, against the background of German occupation. Even more searchingly it is discussed directly by Camus in *L'Homme Révolté*—'I revolt, therefore we are.' Alongside Camus is the whole literature of the 'extreme situation'. Sartre's existentialist view-point was that man must commit himself, act, and accept the consequences. In his play *Les Mains Sales* (published in the U.K. as *Crime Passionel*) the old Communist turns on the scrupulous young idealist:

'How attached to your purity you are, my boy! . . . Purity is an ideal for a fakir or a monk. You intellectuals, you bourgeois anarchists, you use it as an excuse for doing nothing. . . . My hands are filthy. I've dipped them up to the elbows in blood and filth. So what? Do you think that you can govern and keep your spirits white?'[12]

The speaker has committed himself, and it is doubtless no accident that he is the most warm-hearted and convincing person in the play. But when one goes on to ask on what basis one should act, one finds oneself back at the starting point with the question unanswered.

3. 'HELL IS THE OTHERS'

Sartre's play *In Camera* or *No Exit* (*Huis Clos*) shows a vicious circle of three people, dead and looking over the mistaken actions, or inaction, of their lives. The essential feature of their hell is that they must remain for ever shut in with the others. If modern man, however, is fully to know himself, and if he is to act with conviction, this can only be done in relationship to others.

One of the most fundamental links between people is everyday speech, yet patently this can be a very unsatisfactory means of communication. Nuances of social class, personal experience, conscious or unconscious concealment of meaning, all can form a barrier. Thus it is possible for a talkative person to remain isolated, and for members of a conference never, in Buber's sense, to meet. This is the situation which some modern drama has exploited to build up a disturbing picture of men's isolation from each other. In Pinter's play *The Caretaker*, for instance, there are only three characters: a tramp and two brothers. The talk flows endlessly and is often of the most banal kind. Sometimes an individual character talks at great length, almost to himself. And yet at the end of it, they seem to have no greater knowledge of each other, or we of them: only a sharpened sense of the meaninglessness of life and of underlying menace.

If language is one, then sex is another of the fundamental opportunities of relationship between human beings, and a subject that has been almost an obsession of modern writers. Novelists, poets, and dramatists have all explored the tenuous nature of this link—its brevity, its scope for misunderstanding, its aberrations, its possible bitterness. If one thing is certain in modern literature, it is that they will not 'live happily ever after'. And very much the same could be said when the focus is turned on social divisions and race conflicts. The continuous theme has been of the separateness of human beings as the basic condition, and their coming together as only a passing experience. 'Only connect' has been one of E. M. Forster's main themes, and his sad doubts about it can be taken as standing for many:

> '. . . "We may hate one another, but we hate you most. If I don't make you go, Ahmed will, Karim will, if it's fifty-five-hundred years we shall get rid of you, yes, we shall drive every blasted Englishman into the sea, and then"—he rode against him furiously—"and then", he concluded, half kissing him, "you and I shall be friends."
>
> "Why can't we be friends now?" said the other, holding him affectionately. "It's what I want. It's what you want."
>
> But the horses didn't want it—they swerved apart; the earth didn't want it, sending up rocks through which riders must pass single file; the temples, the tank, the jail, the palace, the birds, the carrion, the Guest House, that came into view

as they issued from the gap and saw Mau beneath: they didn't want it, they said in their hundred voices, "No, not yet", and the sky said, "No, not there".[13]

The extreme examples of separation are the wholly isolated individuals—The Outsiders, explored in Colin Wilson's study.[14] Haller in Hesse's *Steppenwolf*, Roquentin in Sartre's *La Nausée*, Mersault in Camus' *L'Etranger*, are all solitary figures who feel outside of, or at least out of tune with, their society.

Such figures may often be regarded as the very opposite of the 'sleepwalkers'. They are not men of the past, automatically carrying out an inherited pattern which is no longer valid in the present. They are, if anything, men of the future, struggling with a life pattern of their own wish and devising, and acutely aware of their own actions. And this is no less true when the modern artist himself is considered as playing the role of outsider. He is misunderstood because his art forms are not yet the accepted and established currency. The archetypal modern artist, indeed, may well be thought of as an exile. Many have been, by wish or by force, actual exiles—Joyce, for instance, Auden, Brecht, Thomas Mann, Picasso, Stravinsky, Kokoschka. Fundamentally they are exiles working in a society, with a strange language and unshared values.

4. NO HERO IN A LANDSCAPE

Heroes are inseparable from their settings. To think of Ulysses is to recall the 'wine-dark sea' of his voyaging; to think of Don Quixote is to picture him on his horse against the sun-dried landscape of Castille. Even boyhood's Robin Hood is inconceivable away from his forest. Perhaps of all these Don Quixote lies closest to our times and is the most disturbing. Unlike the others he is a lonely figure, accompanied only by Sancho Panza and his donkey; and unlike them, he fights not against real things, but against the giants from his own mind. Something has started to go wrong.

Are there any modern heroes at all? Certainly Brecht makes both political and artistic sense when he attacks hero-worship in his audiences: 'Don't gawp so romantically'—as his banner across the stage put it. Again, one feels that the process Marini saw in his own work has a wider reference:

'If you look at my equestrian statues of the last twelve years
in order of time, you will notice that the animal's panic steadily
increases, but that it is frozen with terror and stands paralysed
rather than rearing or taking flight. In every figure, I strove to
express a deepening fear and despair. In this way, I am attempting to symbolize the last stage of a dying myth, the myth
of the individual victorious hero, of the humanist's man of
virtue.'[15]

Of course, the tough men are still there, in spy story (setting:
cosmopolitan), in gangster thriller (setting: urban), in western
(setting: elemental and rocky), whether the tale is told in paperback or celluloid, there are still strong men who kill, and rescue
dames, if not damsels. Some writers, such as Hemingway, have
a fond concern for men of action, springing from a sense that such
a life-pattern is threatened; sea and mountain are now no longer
man's most likely protagonists, and war is no longer a matter of
individual combat: hence *A Farewell to Arms* and the hard heroic
life. One of the places where the epic hero still survives is in the
film—one of several signs that the cinema is both a child of the
twentieth century and one of the most traditional of the modern
arts, tied to narrative, realism and the outsize personality. For
great epic films—probably the most lasting and closest to the saga
—one turns again to Eisenstein's *Alexander Nevsky* and *Ivan the
Terrible*. A society whose ideology stresses the communal has
kept the hero, whereas the 'western' world with its cult of the
individual has lost him.

Perhaps it is just that the individual has taken his place—the
little fellow has become a kind of hero. The West counters Alexander Nevsky battling on the ice against Teutonic Knights with
Charlie Chaplin eating his boot-laces as spaghetti, snowed up in
a gold rush. It has become a world of 'men without qualities'—to
adapt the title of Musil's great work. The Herzog of Saul Bellow,
the Mr. Bloom of Joyce's *Ulysses*, the Hans Castorp of Mann's
Magic Mountain are all ordinary chaps! Here is modern heroism:

'On the doorstep he felt in his hip pocket for the latchkey.
Not there. In the trousers I left off. Must get it. Potato I have.
Creaky wardrobe. No use disturbing her. She turned over
sleepily that time. He pulled the halldoor to after him very
quietly, more, till the footleaf dropped gently over the thresh-

old, a limp lid. Looked shut. All right till I come back any-
how.'[16]

Leopold Bloom has gone out to buy kidneys for breakfast: his
heroic day has begun. Some men may have faced greater odds
than cooking kidneys, but are heroic only in that they have survived, not that they have altered the situation. Joyce himself in
A Portrait of the Artist as a Young Man saw his rôle as that of
'silence, exile, and cunning', if he was to keep himself intact as a
writer. Mother Courage, peddling her goods to both sides in the
Thirty Years' War, has a ruthless 'save myself' policy, even to the
point of denying her son. Billy Liar and Arthur Seaton, whether
working in a factory or out on Saturday night, get by with a
bouncy cynicism and self-confidence, which puts them in the sun
sexually if not socially. Recent American fiction also has a good
crop of such individualists:

> 'Don't talk to me about fighting to save my country. I've
> been fighting all along to save my country. Now I'm going to
> fight a little to save myself. The country's not in danger any
> more, but I am. . . . From now on I'm thinking only of me.'
> (Yossarian in Joseph Heller's *Catch-22*)

Or those who withdraw, and make themselves outsiders:

> 'My hole is warm and full of light. Yes, *full* of light. I doubt
> if there is a brighter spot in all New York. . . . I tapped a
> power-line leading into the building and ran it into my hole in
> the ground. . . . And so I play the invisible music of my isola-
> tion.' (Ralph Ellison's *Invisible Man*)

More pathetic and more extreme is the college baseball hero of
John Updike's *Run, Rabbit, Run,* who, faced with the problems of
real life, finds them beyond him and does just that—runs:

> 'His hands lift of their own and he feels the wind on his
> ears even before, his heels hitting heavily on the pavement at
> first but with an effortless gathering out of a kind of sweet
> panic growing lighter and quicker and quieter, he runs. Ah!
> runs. Runs.'[17]

One has moved into the tragic, but modern art offers victims
rather than tragic heroes as Shakespeare or the Greeks knew

them. Willy Lomax in Arthur Miller's *Death of a Salesman* falls a victim to a vicious business system, and Dr. Zhivago disintegrates as a person in a society which constrained the individual and upheld collective values. More sinister is the fate of K in Kafka's *The Trial* or *The Castle*. He is the victim of a situation which he cannot understand, because the knowledge available is contradictory, which makes him feel guilty, although he has done no known wrong, and against which he cannot appeal because there is no chance to communicate with the authorities.

Don Quixote moved freely in a landscape. The sheep and windmills were hostile only in his own mind, not in any reality known to Sancho Panza. Modern art suggests a more ominous setting for man, whether he is a hero or not.

Man, indeed, may be in a trap. Kafka's K is trapped in the village, and will never be able to enter the Castle. Sartre's characters, caught in their vicious circle, are also held within the four walls of a room. The central character of Canetti's *Auto-Da-Fé* is a prisoner, as it were, within his library. Bacon's Pope seems fixed in some enclosed space. The figures in some of Henry Moore's drawings are bound in by walls, relieved only by narrow slits, or trapped in the tunnel of a London Underground.

A tunnel, however, could be regarded as protective, even with possibilities of rebirth. Giorgio di Chirico used the material world in his paintings to convey a sense of menace. 'Every object', he said, 'has two aspects: the common aspect, which is the one we generally see and which is seen by everyone, and the ghostly and metaphysical aspect, which only rare individuals see.' This latter reality he expressed 'in a panic-stricken rigidity, and the atmosphere of the pictures is one of nightmare and of fathomless melancholy. The city squares of Italy, the towers and objects, are set in an over-acute perspective, as if they were in a vacuum, illuminated by a merciless, cold light from an unseen source.'[18] He painted what he believed Schopenhauer and Nietzsche to have discovered—'a dreadful void'.

For other men that void was the desert. This might mean the vast open spaces of the Australian out-back across which Sidney Nolan's *Ned Kelly* rides, in his angular iron mask, hunted by the police. More likely and more hostile is the desert of Patrick White's *Voss*, as he and his little party pressed into the Australian continent '. . . riding eternally over the humped and hateful earth, which the sun had seared until the spent and crumbly stuff was become highly treacherous.'[19] Again, Sutherland's thorns have more than a hint of the desert, and much modern painting, as has been said, is barren of people.

Men, however, may fill great cities, but they too know the void of Auden's *Age of Anxiety*, or are plague-stricken as in Camus' *The Plague*. And their busyness may express emptiness:

'Unreal City,
Under the brown fog of a winter dawn,
A crowd flowed over London Bridge, so many,
I had not thought death had undone so many.'[20]

The landscape of the modern arts remains unchanging between Eliot's 'The Waste Land', where no water is found, to the derelict ground of Beckett's *Waiting for Godot* to which Godot never comes.

REFERENCES

1. ELIOT, T. S.: *Collected Poems, 1909–1935* (Faber, 1936). From the poem 'The Hollow Men', pp. 89–90.*

2. WEISS, P.: *The Persecution and Assassination of Marat as performed by the inmates of the asylum of Charenton under the direction of the Marquis of Sade.* Tr. G. Shelton (Calder, 1965).*

3. BACON, F.: Quoted from RUSSELL, J.: *Francis Bacon* (Methuen, 'Art in Progress' series, 1964), Introduction.

4. BRECHT, B.: From *Four Psalms.* Quoted from ESSLIN, M.: *Brecht: A Choice of Evils* (Eyre and Spottiswoode, 1959), p. 227.*

5. MOORE, H.: *Henry Moore on Sculpture*, op. cit. From his introductory pamphlet for his 'Madonna and Child' at Northampton, 1943–44, p. 220.

6. NEUMANN, E.: *The Archetypal World of Henry Moore.* Tr. Hull (Routledge, 1959), pp. 128–9.*

7. BROCH, H.: *The Sleepwalkers.* Tr. by Willa and Edwin Muir (Secker, 1939).*

8. BRECHT, B.: Quoted from ESSLIN, M., op. cit., p. 221.

9. AICHINGER, I.: *The Bound Man.* Tr. E. Mosbacher (Secker, 1955), p. 1.*

10. BERGENGRUEN, W.: *A Matter of Conscience.* Tr. N. Cameron (Thames and Hudson, 1952), p. 8.

11. BRECHT, B.: *The Life of Galileo.* Tr. D. I. Vesey (Methuen's Modern Plays, 1963), p. 118.
12. SARTRE, J. P.: *Crime Passionel (Les Mains Sales)*, published in the U.S. as *Dirty Hands*, in *Three Plays*. Tr by K. Black (Hamish Hamilton, 1949), p. 85.*
13. FORSTER, E. M.: *Passage to India* (Penguin Modern Classics), p. 317.*
14. WILSON, C.: *The Outsider* (Gollancz, 1956).*
15. MARINI, M.: Quoted from JUNG, C. G., op. cit. (Aniela Jaffé), p. 266.
16. JOYCE, J.: *Ulysses* (Bodley Head. New ed., 1960), p. 67.*
17. HELLER, J.: *Catch-22* (Cape, 1962. Also Corgi). Bombardier Yossarian was often less decorous: 'Am I supposed to get my ass shot off just because the colonel wants to be a general?' (p. 121. Cape).*
    ELLISON, R.: *The Invisible Man* (Penguin Modern Classics), pp. 9, 15.
    UPDIKE, J.: *Run, Rabbit, Run* (Penguin, p. 249).*
    See the article 'Anathematizing the Asylum' (*Times Literary Supplement*, November 25, 1965), in which the first two passages are quoted.
18. JAFFÉ, A.: Quoted, together with Chirico's statement from JUNG, C. G., op. cit., pp. 254–5.
19. WHITE, P.: *Voss* (Penguin Modern Classics), p. 210.* The cover design is by Sidney Nolan. For the Ned Kelly series, see MELVILLE, R.: *Ned Kelly—27 paintings by Sidney Nolan* (Thames and Hudson, 1964).*
20. ELIOT, T. S.: 'The Waste Land,' op. cit.

CHAPTER TWO

Living Through Change

'THE history of England', wrote Macaulay, 'is emphatically the history of progress.'[1] 'Progress, therefore,' echoed the sociologist Spencer, 'is not an accident, but a necessity. It is part of nature.'[2] It was easy for Tennyson to call:

'. . . Forward, forward let us range,
Let the great world spin for ever down the ringing grooves of change.'[3]

Not all their contemporaries, however, agreed. Some were sad and disturbed, as they saw, like Arnold, the Sea of Faith retreating:

'. . . down the vast edges drear
And naked shingles of the world.'[4]

Yet for the arts, to be stretched between such optimism and doubt seemed a stimulus for narrative, in novel, opera, poem, and painting. The dark and the light only gave force to the story.

The twentieth century offered catastrophes of such dimensions that the human story, it seemed, shuddered into meaninglessness, under threat of extinction. 'Stop the world!' cried the clown, 'I want to get off.'

I. SCRUTINY OF THE PRESENT

If one could no longer believe that change meant progress, one was forced to scrutinize more sharply than ever before what was going on in the present. There was an urgent practical need to find out what was happening and to assess its significance. Such

77

an enquiry was congenial to modern man with his sharp analytical mind, and sociology and economics have flourished.

An artist, however, equally concerned to probe, was less likely to do so with statistics. Freud, with his exploration of man's irrational side determining his actions, was a more likely ally. This was one of the sources of the 'stream of consciousness' novel.

The 'stream of consciousness' novel, as the name suggests, was concerned with the immediate reflections of an individual on his environment, with what was happening, both outside and inside himself. Quite simply the plot was his flow of thoughts. Inevitably, such a flow is haphazard, and this results in a total break from the narrative line of the nineteenth-century novel. Moreover, it involves the over-lapping of considerations of time; one's thoughts in the present are loaded with the past and formative for the future, albeit in the erratic, partly unconscious, way such thinking has. All time becomes present. Not least, such a procedure has one great advantage for the novelist: as consciousness is essentially personal and inward, it enables the novelist to pursue his scrutiny on his own imaginative ground, and not as a sociologist's analysis from the outside.

Since the whole of life may be in such a flow, it is not surprising that such novels are amorphous and offer a wide range of qualities. Some of the high points of Virginia Woolf, for example, are moments of exquisite sense perception:

'. . . up above, here in my serene head, come only fine gusts of melody, waves of incense, while the lost dove wails, and the banners tremble above tombs, and the dark airs of midnight shake trees outside the open windows. When I look down from this transcendency, how beautiful are even the crumbled relics of bread! What shapely spirals the peelings of pears make—how thin, and mottled like some sea-bird's eggs. Even the forks laid straight side by side appear lucid, logical, exact; and the horns of the rolls which we have left are glazed, yellow-plated, hard. I could worship my hand even, with its fan of bones laced by blue mysterious veins and its astonishing look of aptness, suppleness and ability to curl softly or suddenly crush—its infinite sensibility. . . .'[5]

With Hermann Broch, some of the outstanding passages are of

imaginative reflection. His long novel *The Death of Virgil* is the sustained inner monologue of the poet's thoughts during the last hours of his life:

'. . . Nevertheless human life was thus image-graced and image-cursed; it could be comprehended only through images, the images were not to be banished, they had been with us since the herd-beginning, they were anterior to and mightier than our thinking, they were timeless containing past and future, they were a two-fold dream memory and they were more powerful than we: an image to himself was he who lay there, and steering toward the most real reality, borne on invisible waves, dipping into them, the image of the ship was his own image emerging from the darkness, heading towards darkness sinking into darkness, he himself was the boundless ship that at the same time was boundlessness; and he himself was the flight that was aiming toward this boundlessness; he was the fleeing ship, he himself the goal, he himself was boundlessness too vast to be seen, unimaginable, an endless corporeal landscape, the landscape of his body, a mighty, outspread, infernal image of night, so that deprived of the unity of human life, deprived of the unity of human yearning, he no longer believed himself capable of self-mastery, conscious as he was of the separated regions and provinces over which the essential ego had been compelled to distribute itself, conscious of a demonic possession, that had assumed direction in his stead, isolated into districts in all their diversity; ah there were the isolated, ploughed-up districts of the hurting lung. . . . (His thoughts wander over the various parts of his body and their meaning.) . . . all these domains of the physical and extra-physical, enveloping the hard and earthly reality of the skeleton, they were known to him in their complete strangeness, in their disintegrated fragility, in their remoteness, in their animosity, in their incomprehensible infinity, sensual and supra-sensual, for all together, and he along with them as by their mutual knowledge, were imbedded in that great flood that extended over everything human, everything oceanic, in that homing surge and the heavy swing of its ebb and flow which beats so constantly on the coast of the heart and keeps it throbbing so continuously, image of reality and reality of image in one, so wave-deep that most disparate things are swept together within it, not quite unified but still united for future rebirth; oh surf on the shore of cognition, its ever-mounting tide brimming with the seeds of all comfort, all hope, oh, night-laden, seed-laden, space-laden flood of spring; and filled with the empowering vision of his real self, he knew that the demoniac could be overcome through the assurance of reality, the image of which lies in the province of the indescribable yet nonetheless contains the unity of the world.'[6]

This is one of the extremely long sentences from the Adagio section of the novel, for Broch planned the four sections (*Water—the Arrival*; *Fire—the Descent*; *Earth—the Expectation*; *Air—the Homecoming*), with symphonic form in mind. He realized, as did Joyce, that both in its form and its use of language there was an affinity between the 'stream of consciousness' novel and music. There is also a link between such novels and the work of the visual artists: in the early experiments, for instance, of Picasso and Braque, the reality of an object, such as a violin, is conveyed by an amalgam of disconnected parts, aspects which an observer would be aware of from different angles and over a period of time. The unified view, in perspective, like the continuous narrative of the novel, has become fragmented, in a way that gives a sharper and fuller idea of its reality.

In some ways, the fullest common ground exists between such novels and the cinema. This was pointed out by Hauser in his *Social History of Art*. He discusses our ideas of time:

'The time experience of the present age consists above all in an awareness of the moment in which we find ourselves: in an awareness of the present.

'The new concept of time, whose basic element is simultaneity and whose nature consists in the spatialization of the temporal element, is expressed in no other genre so impressively as in this youngest art, which dates from the same period as Bergson's philosophy of time.'

And he relates this interest in simultaneity to the montage technique of short-cutting:

'. . . no longer the phenomena of a homogeneous world of objects, but of quite heterogeneous elements of reality that were brought face to face. Thus Eisenstein showed the following sequence in *The Battleship Potemkin*: men working desperately, engine room of the cruiser; busy hands, revolving wheels; faces distorted with exertion; maximum pressure of the manometer; a chest soaked with perspiration, a glowing boiler; an arm, a wheel; a wheel, an arm; machine, man; machine, man; machine, man.'[7]

Quite apart from short-cutting to show the facets of a situation, the cinema can also show events happening simultaneously in other places. Girl tied to the line, mile away a train approaching; across the prairie hero riding to rescue—audience kept in touch with each situation. Yet this banal example points to a basic difference between the cinema and the 'stream of consciousness' novel—the cinema uses this technique to increase the intensity of the story, whereas the novel breaks the narrative line.

It was a possible danger of such novels that they offered only a ramble of sense impressions, and of the cinema that its juxtaposition of vivid glimpses only aided the telling of a melodrama. But perhaps they both helped to show the complexity of the present in any individual's awareness. This fascination with 'a lifetime burning in every moment' led some artists to explore more fully and deeply the problem of time.

2. THE MOMENT OF TIME

Perhaps it would be better to say that they were fascinated less by the complexity of the present, than by the potential significance of a single instant.

> 'Not the intense moment
> Isolated, with no before or after,
> But a lifetime burning in every moment.'[8]

If eternity could be found in Blake's grain of sand, so could the whole meaning of the past, present, and future be caught in a single moment.

One great connoisseur of such moments was Marcel Proust. Early in his many-volumed attempt to rebuild a time that has gone, he tells of the excitement roused in him by drinking a cup of tea:

'No sooner had the warm liquid, and the crumbs with it, touched my palate than a shudder ran through my whole body, and I stopped, intent upon the extraordinary changes that were taking place. An exquisite pleasure had invaded my senses, but individual, detached, with no suggestion of its origin.'

He probes to find why. He drinks again, and yet again, but this does not help. 'It is plain that the object of my quest, the truth, lies not in the cup but in myself.' But how could he seize it?

'What an abyss of uncertainty whenever the mind feels that some part of it has strayed beyond its own borders; when it, the seeker, is at once the dark region through which it must go on seeking, where all its equipment will avail it nothing. Seek? More than that: create. It is face to face with something which does not so far exist, to which it can alone give reality and sub-stance, which it alone can bring into the light of day.'
And he goes on reflecting at length:
'Will it ultimately reach the clear surface of my conscious-ness, this memory, this old, dead moment which the magnetism of an identical moment has travelled so far to importune, to disturb, to raise out of the very depths of my being?
'. . . And suddenly the memory returns. The taste was that of the little crumb of madeleine which on Sunday mornings at Combray . . . my aunt Leonie used to give me, dipping it first in her own cup of real or of lime-flower tea.'[9]

From there the recollection of that moment fans out into the reconstruction of all his childhood visits.
In a sense, however, the significance of such moments to him is functional: they focus a whole series of memories and are open to infinite elaboration. They are not the moments 'in and out of time' which are one of the *leitmotifs* of Eliot's *Four Quartets*; nor is their significance the same. Eliot was concerned with the re-demption of the human situation, but he refused to see this in any secular view of man's activity in a sequence of time. 'If all time is eternally present,' he said, at least in the sociological sense of the present determined by the past and man's present plans shaping the future, then 'all time is unredeemable.' Eliot, as a religious man, believed only in salvation at those points where the eternal

cut across the temporal, as a Christian would believe happened at the Crucifixion. History was a 'pattern of timeless moments.'

> '. . . But to apprehend
> The point of intersection of the timeless
> With time, is an occupation for the saint—
> No occupation either, but something given
> And taken, in a lifetime's death in love,
> Ardour and selflessness and self-surrender.'

Clearly, this intersection is something very much more than Proust's key moments of recollection, and it is not, as Eliot recognized, a normal experience:

> 'For most of us, there is only the unattended
> Moment, the moment in and out of time,
> The distraction fit, lost in a shaft of sunlight,
> The wild thyme unseen, or the winter lightning.
> Or the waterfall, or music heard so deeply
> That it is not heard at all, but you are the music
> While the music lasts. These are only hints and guesses. . . .'[10]

One is interested to find another modern poet, Jiminez, describing just such a moment:

> 'Flowering and living, the moment of a central spark, prolonged and open in a tempting form; a moment with no past, in which the four points of the compass exert equal attraction, both sweet and deep, a moment of love open like a flower. Love and flower in perfect form.'[11]

Different again is the emphasis of Rilke. He was concerned less with such moments, visualized as a point in time, as with a certain quality of being. This quality was achieved by making living a kind of poetic creativeness, and it was the essence of such creativity to break down divisions—between outward and inward, the real and the imagined, life and death—in short, to achieve what Eliot called 'the impossible union of spheres of existence'.

> 'There outside is everything that I am experiencing within, and nothing has limit either within or without; only that I weave myself more closely into things when my glance harmonizes with them, and with the serious simplicity of their

shapes—then the earth outgrows itself. It seems to enclose the whole sky; the first star is like the last house.'[12]

But such perception and living was only possible if men would accept being changed. Where Eliot talked of redemption, Rilke is concerned with transformation, with metamorphosis:

'*Wolle die Wandlung*.'—'Aspire to be changed!'

It is perhaps inevitable that in describing the moments 'out of time' one has called on the poets. Any painter, however, who uses symbols perceptively may be trying to make the grain of sand, as it were, express the eternal. Chagall, for instance, uses symbols drawn from his early life in Russia and from Jewry to express his belief in the transcendent, and sometimes comes surprisingly close to Rilke.

> 'All these planes of God's hidden world become visible in Chagall's pictures; they appear in the natural, that is, divine intermixture that determines the world of the soul: natural thing and symbol; spectre and reality; harlequinade of life and lovers' magic; naked drive and religious ecstasy; pillaging soldiers and the silver, fish-tailed dancer of the soul; trumpets of judgement and the endless train of mothers with child, of Marys on the flight to Egypt; the apocalyptic end of the world and the October Revolution; scrolls of the Torah, crucifixes, candelabra, cackling hens, ecstatic asses, and radiant violins whose music hovers between heaven and earth. And over and over again the moon. The godhead speaks in colours and symbols.'[13]

So poet and painter. The composer Michael Tippett has also questioned the possibility of using his medium to express 'the poetical, theatrical moment which is out of time and beyond death'. He feels that music could more easily be used in this way in the past when a primitive, hieratic sense was still potent, than in a modern technological society. The starting point of his questioning was Yeats' stage direction asking for the music of 'Drum, Flute and Zither',[14] at the unbearable moment of tragedy when the Irish hero realizes he has killed his own son. Could music take the place of words in such moments of 'life enflamed by death'?

3. THE BACKWARD LOOK

'The backward look behind the assurance
Of recorded history, the backward half-look
Over the shoulder, towards the primitive terror.' (Eliot)[15]

'. . . I soon realized that spiritually life in the mere present is insupportable and senseless, and that a spiritual life is made possible only by a steadfast relationship with the past, with history and with the old and age-old. . . .' (Hesse)[16]

Every period looks back to the past for a different need and looks with different eyes. A man may look at the same past as a previous generation, but will be asking other questions and finding other answers. The last hundred years has seen not only a more rigorously academic approach to history, not only the unearthing of a mass of new evidence—not least about the remote past, but also the emergence of a world ideology, based on a particular interpretation of history. No artist can remain unaware of this changed thought-world or of this knowledge; indeed he, too, in his art may find an acute need to turn to the past.

Out of such a need arose the use of Greek myth already mentioned; but it will be more useful here to limit the past to more recent and firmly recorded times, and to the past of the artist's own nation or society. Such is the past of the epic, and in it one may see the poet serving as historian for his people. The epic appealed to the pride of the group, recorded heroic action, was enjoyed by the group as an emotional experience and was sustained by a common body of values. It may serve as an illustration to suggest that Eisenstein's historical films are epics, whereas Brecht's historical plays are not. A film such as *Alexander Nevsky* upholds the pride of the Russians through the hero's defeat of the Germanic invader; it shows the kind of heroism Russia needed to resist Hitler; it could be experienced by mass audiences, with Prokofiev's music heightening the emotion; and—perhaps less clearly—it was nourished by the ideology of Communism. Brecht, however, is different. He is anti-heroic, as in *Galileo*. He deliberately plans to alienate his audiences, refusing to allow them to be emotionally involved, so that they can critically assess the human situation before them. He wrote for no clearly defined audience, and his underlying purpose is more often guided by the poet in

him than the communist. Yet Brecht's use of history was not
accidental: it enabled his audiences to stand back from a situation,
so that they could scrutinize events, which were parallel to but
apart from their contemporary experience.

One could start the other way round and ask: what present
experiences and what needs have stimulated artists to turn to the
past of their society? A good example comes from Japan. In 1945,
Japan experienced a catastrophic defeat. A form of national identity, symbolized by the person and sanctity of the Emperor,
seemed destroyed, and world public opinion condemned the
Japanese as sub-human. It can be suggested that in such a situation, they turned to an art-form in which they were strong—
the cinema—and that some directors created films which portrayed a time when a way of life, truly and distinctively Japanese,
was still intact. They were, however, portraits with an underlying
questioning. So Japan now has the largest film industry in the
world, and a world reputation for historical films: films such as
Kurosawa's *Throne of Blood*, *The Seven Samurai* and *Rashomon*[17]
and Mizoguchi's *Ugetsu Monogatari*.

It is possible also to suggest that against the unhappy experiences of Germany since the First World War, German artists
have used an art-form in which they were nationally strong—the
opera—and drawn on their own history for themes, as did Hindemith in *Mathis der Maler*—a study of the agonized Matthias
Grünewald in the disturbed sixteenth century. At least three
composers have actually used earlier German dramas for plots—
Berg in *Wozzeck*, Henze in *The Prince of Homburg*, and Klebe in
Die Räuber; while sometimes there has been a return to the fantasy
world of the Brothers Grimm, such as in Henze's *König Hirsch*
or Egk's *Die Zaubergeige*. Thus can the past aid a re-discovery of
identity.

History, however, can also be used to make a commentary on
the present. One particularly sharp-edged example is Robert
Lowell's poem 'For the Union Dead'. Here was a very difficult
thing for a poet to do: namely to take an area of his country's past
so recent and deeply felt as the American Civil War and use it to
imply criticisms of modern American society and policies, especially over the position of the Negro. Its power is increased by its
many-textured quality, giving references to both a fuller history
—the long forgotten dinosaur, his own personal story, the strong

tradition of New England puritanism, the close memory of
Hiroshima—as well as to the natural world in contrast to man's
beastliness—bird, animal, reptile, and, above all, fish. To use his
own image, such a poem sticks in the throat like a fishbone. Its
essential background is the Civil Rights Movement, and it may
be regarded as the artistic expression of views which Lowell has
privately shown in his imprisonment as a pacifist in the Second
World War, and his recent refusal to attend a White House
function because of his dislike of America's policy in Vietnam. It
is best to let the poem speak for itself.[18]

FOR THE UNION DEAD
'Relinquunt omnia servare rem publicam'

The old South Boston Aquarium stands
in a Sahara of snow now. Its broken windows are boarded.
The bronze weathervane cod has lost half its scales.
The airy tanks are dry.

Once my nose crawled like a snail on the glass;
my hand tingled
to burst the bubbles
drifting from the noses of the cowed, compliant fish.

My hand draws back. I often sigh still
for the dark downward and vegetating kingdom
of the fish and reptile. One morning last March,
I pressed against the new barbed and galvanized

fence on the Boston Common. Behind their cage,
yellow dinosaur steamshovels were grunting
as they cropped up tons of mush and grass
to gouge their underworld garage.

Parking spaces luxuriate like civic
sandpiles in the heart of Boston.
A girdle of orange, Puritan-pumpkin coloured girders
braces the tingling Statehouse,

shaking over the excavations, as it faces Colonel Shaw
and his bell-cheeked infantry
on St. Gaudens' shaking Civil War relief,
propped by a plank splint against the garage's earthquake.

Two months after marching through Boston,
half the regiment was dead;
at the dedication,
William James could almost hear the bronze Negroes breathe.

Their monument sticks like a fishbone
in the city's throat.
Its Colonel is as lean
as a compass-needle.

He has an angry wrenlike vigilance,
a greyhound's gentle tautness;
he seems to wince at pleasure,
and suffocate for privacy.

He is out of bounds now. He rejoices in man's lovely,
peculiar power to choose life and die—
when he leads his black soldiers to death,
he cannot bend his back.

On a thousand New England greens,
the old white churches hold their air
of sparse, sincere rebellion; frayed flags
quilt the graveyards of the Grand Army of the Republic.

The stone statues of the abstract Union Soldier
grow slimmer and younger each year—
wasp-waisted, they doze over muskets
and muse through their sideburns. . . .

Shaw's father wanted no monument
except the ditch,
where his son's body was thrown
and lost with his 'niggers'.

The ditch is nearer.
There are no statues for the last war here;
on Boylston Street, a commercial photograph
shows Hiroshima boiling

over a Mosler Safe, the 'Rock of Ages'
that survived the blast. Space is nearer.
When I crouch to my television set,
the drained faces of Negro school-children rise like balloons.

Colonel Shaw
is riding on his bubble,
he waits
for the blessed break.

The Aquarium is gone. Everywhere,
giant finned cars nose forward like fish;
a savage servility
slides by on grease.

4. THE EVENT

Almost without realizing it one has moved into the artist's involvement in contemporary events. Faced with the public life of
our time—wars, slumps, conflicts, changes—what is to be the
artist's answer? Need indeed the artist offer any at all? If he allows
it, how can his experience of contemporary political life express
itself in his art?

One response is to record it. Not as a journalist wanting vivid
copy for a wider public, and satisfied with outward narrative,
but rather under the sharpened sense that here was a catastrophic
experience, deeply affecting the lives of a generation, and, if only
for the writer's own need of understanding, some attempt to
record it was essential. Perhaps inevitably the novel comes to the
fore. To give some examples:

Arnold Zweig: *The Case of Sergeant Grischa.* ⎤   (First
Ludwig Renn: *Krieg.* (War)   ⎦   World War)
Pasternak: *Dr. Zhivago.*
Babel: *Red Cavalry.*   ⎱ (Russian Revolution)
Sholokhov: *And Quiet Flows the Don.* ⎰
Malraux: *La Condition Humaine.* (Communist activity in China
in the 1920's)
Steinbeck: *The Grapes of Wrath.* (America of Roosevelt's New
Deal)
Hemingway: *For Whom the Bell Tolls.* (Spanish Civil War)
Koestler: *Darkness at Noon.* (Stalin's Treason Trials)
Sartre: *The Reprieve.* (The Munich Crisis, 1938)
    Iron in the Soul. (Fall of France)

Mailer: *The Naked and the Dead*. (Second World War)
Mann: *Dr. Faustus*. (Hitler's Germany)

Yet such a list—quite apart from its arbitrary nature—raises doubts and questions. Some of these books might be considered as too light-weight to last. Several writers of undisputed stature—Lawrence, Joyce, and Kafka—are not included because their work does not touch on political events. Again there seems to be no tie up between what an historian and a novelist would regard as important: from the historian's view-point outstanding events are missed out, while the novelist busies himself with some individual in a side-track. Moreover, as with Mann and Sartre, the actual historical setting or event are no more than a background to a complex philosophical enquiry. One wonders whether, after all, the novel is the best recording medium. Thinking only of the First World War, and keeping to British artists alone, one can offer Paul Nash's paintings, such as *The Menin Road* or *Sanctuary Wood, Dawn*, the poetry of Wilfred Owen, David Jones's play *In Parenthesis*, and Robert Graves' autobiography, *Goodbye To All That*—all giving one sharp insights into the experience of that war, and all war. Nevertheless it remains open to question whether artists may not be too close to the experience to describe it, on the analogy of Tolstoy's *War and Peace*, written many years after an historical event in which he did not even take part.

There have been events of the modern world, however, in which artists have very much taken part, and held a committed position, using their art as a weapon in the conflict, as has already been seen in Lowell's poem. The Spanish Civil War drove Picasso to paint *Guernica*, with its agonized forms, in anger against the inhumanity of the first obliteration bombing. Out of this war too came George Orwell's *Homage to Catalonia*, Koestler's *Spanish Testament*, Barea's *The Clash*, Malraux's *L'Espoir*, Hemingway's *For Whom the Bell Tolls*, Brecht's *Señor Carrara's Rifles*, and the anthology *Poems for Spain* (1939) which showed the involvement of a whole generation of young English poets. The German occupation of France raised a special problem for writers: to protest and yet to survive. Rarely has the pressure to communicate with their fellows seemed more urgent. This gave rise to such works as Sartre's *The Flies* and *Huis Clos*, Anouilh's *The Lark*, and *Antigone* and Camus's *The Plague*. The approach is indirect

—allegory, analogy, inference—yet each expresses the terrible experience of occupation from within that experience.

The experience of the artist is unlikely to be the rational one of political comment, and the stimulus to creativity may lie deeper than the event. As Wilfred Owen wrote:

> 'This book is not about heroes. English poetry is not yet fit to speak of them.
>
> 'Nor is it about deeds, or lands, nor anything about glory, honour, might, majesty, dominion, or power, except War.
>
> 'Above all I am not concerned with Poetry.
>
> 'My subject is War, and the pity of War.
>
> 'The Poetry is in the pity.
>
> 'Yet these elegies are to this generation in no sense consolatory. They may be to the next. All a poet can do today is warn. That is why the true poets must be truthful.'[19]

For pity, poetry seems a better medium than prose. The visual arts, too, can arouse pity, as do the long series of Rouault's *Miserere* prints, based on the suffering of the First World War, with their sharp-edged titles—'War, which all mothers hate', 'My sweet homeland, what has become of you?', 'Jesus will be in agony till the end of the world', 'This will be the last time, little father'. Perhaps such feelings find their fullest and deepest expression in music. Schoenberg's *A Survivor from Warsaw*, Dallapiccola's *The Prisoner* and his canticle on Hiroshima, Benjamin Britten's *War Requiem* all express the tragic nature of modern man's political experience. So too does Michael Tippett's oratorio *A Child of Our Time*. Tippett's oratorio is based on an actual incident, when a Jewish boy, driven to desperation for his mother, shot a German diplomat and provoked an intensified persecution of the Jews. Tippett summarized its structure thus:

> 'Part I deals only with the general state of affairs in the world today as it effects all individuals, minorities, classes or races who are felt to be outside the ruling conventions—Man at odds with his Shadow. In Part II appears the Child of Our Time, enmeshed in the drama of his personal fate and the elemental social forces of our day. The drama is due to the fact that the forces which drive the young man prove stronger than the good advice of his uncle and aunt—as it always was and will be.

Part III is concerned with the significance of this drama and
the possible healing that would come from Man's acceptance of
his Shadow in relation to his Light.'[20]

Clearly Tippett is using music here, as Moore used sculpture,
to explore the archetypal situation, beyond and beneath the event.
The experience, as Schoenberg said in another context, is all in
the music, but a slight hint of the work may be gained from some
of the outline of Part II:

> No. 16 *Chorus with solo soprano and tenor.*
> Spiritual II: 'Nobody knows the trouble I see, Lord'.
> No. 17 *Bass and Contralto.*
> The bass sings in recitative style and the contralto comments:
> Bass: 'The boy becomes desperate in his agony.'
> Alto: 'A curse is born. The dark forces threaten him.'
> Bass: 'He goes to authority. He is met with hostility.'
> Alto: 'His other self rises in him, demonic and destructive.'
> Bass: 'He shoots the official.'
> No. 18 *Bass 'The Narrator!'*
> Recitative: 'They took a terrible vengeance'.
> No. 19 *Chorus 'The Terror'.*
> Allegro Molto. Fugal entries. 'Burn down their houses. Beat in
> their heads. Break them in pieces on the wheel.'
> No. 20 *Bass.*
> 'Men were ashamed of what was done. There was bitterness
> and horror.'
> No. 21 *Chorus with Bass solo 'A Spiritual of Anger'.*
> Spiritual III: 'Go down, Moses, way down to Egypt land; tell
> old Pharaoh to let my people go!'[20]

Such an incident was only a detail of the biggest massacre of
the Jews in the whole of human history. One cannot evade the
question: how much horror can art carry? George Steiner raises
this problem in *The Death of Tragedy*. His immediate subject
was drama, but his thoughts have a wider reference:

> 'The political inhumanity of our time has demeaned and
> brutalized language beyond any precedent. . . . Compared with
> the realities of war and oppression that surround us, the
> gravest imaginings of the poets are diminished to a scale of
> private or artificial terror. In *The Trojan Woman* Euripides had

the poetic authority to convey to the Athenian audience the injustice and reproach of the sack of Melos. Cruelty was still commensurate to the scope or response of the imagination.

'I wonder whether this is still the case. What work of art could give adequate expression to our immediate past? The last war has had neither its *Iliad* nor its *War and Peace*. None who have dealt with it have matched the control of remembrance achieved by Robert Graves or Sassoon in their accounts of 1914–18. Language seems to choke on the facts. The only array of words still able to get near the quick of feeling is the kind of naked and prosaic record set down in *The Diary of Anne Frank*.'[21]

REFERENCES

1. MACAULAY, T. B.: *Historical Essays* (In review of Mackintosh's *History of the Revolution*, contributed to the *Edinburgh Review*).*
2. SPENCER, H.: *Social Statics*, Pt. i, chapter 2, § 4.
3. TENNYSON, ALFRED: 'Locksley Hall', lines 181–2.
4. ARNOLD, MATTHEW: 'Dover Beach'.
5. WOOLF, V.: *The Waves* (Penguin Modern Classics), p. 250.*
6. BROCH, H.: *The Death of Virgil* (From Part Two: *Fire—The Descent*). Tr. J. S. Untermeyer (Routledge, 1946), pp. 76–8.*
7. HAUSER, A.: *The Social History of Art*. Tr. S. Goodman (Routledge, 1963. Also paperback). From chapter VIII—'The Film Age' —pp. 939, 954.*
8. ELIOT, T. S.: *Four Quartets*, op. cit. From 'East Coker'.
9. PROUST, M.: *Swann's Way*. Tr. C. K. Scott Moncrieff (Chatto & Windus. Phoenix Library, 1929), pp. 58–61.*
10. ELIOT, T. S.: *Four Quartets*, op. cit. From 'The Dry Salvages'.
11. JIMINEZ, J. R.: Quoted from COHEN, J. M.: *Poetry of this Age, 1908–1958* (Hutchinson University Library, 1966), p. 65. From the poem, 'Flower that returns'.
12. RILKE, R. M.: *Picture Book*. Quoted from COHEN, J. M., op. cit., p. 47. From Rilke's poem 'The Reader'.
13. NEUMANN, E.: *Art, the Creative Unconscious*, op. cit., p. 144. Chagall himself talks of 'a mysterious fourth or fifth dimension . . . which intuitively gives birth to a scale of plastic and psychic contrasts'.
14. TIPPETT, M.: *Moving into Aquarius* (Routledge, 1959). See the essay of that title, 'Drum, Flute and Zither'. Tippett explains that 'drum, flute and zither are emblematic of rhythm, of melody and

of accompaniment . . . a kind of theatrical ritual' (p. 68). He discusses Yeats' play *The Death of Cuchulain*—his last work before his death in 1939. Yeats had explored the same tragic situation in his play *On Baile's Stand* as early as 1901. Both plays can be found in JEFFARES, A. N.: *Yeats: Selected Plays* (Macmillan, St. Martin's Library, 1964).

15. ELIOT, T. S.: *Four Quartets*, op. cit. From 'The Dry Salvages'.

16. HESSE, H.: *A Life in Brief*. Contained in *The Golden Horizon*, edited by Cyril Connolly (Weidenfeld & Nicolson, 1953), p. 289.

17. For the films of Akira Kurosawa, see the recent study by Donald Richie (Cambridge, 1966).*

18. LOWELL, R.: *Selected Poems* (Faber, 1965. Paperback).*

19. OWEN, W.: *The Poems of Wilfrid Owen*. Edited with a memoir and notes by Edmund Blunden (Chatto & Windus, 1946). From Owen's own preface, pp. 40–1.*

20. TIPPETT, M.: *A Child of Our Time*. Quoted from the sleeve of the records, LLC 30114–5 (Pye), of the performance of this work by the Royal Liverpool Philharmonic Orchestra and Choir conducted by John Pritchard. Sleeve notes by John Amis.

21. STEINER, G.: *The Death of Tragedy* (Faber, 1961), pp. 315–16.*

CHAPTER THREE

The World Dialogue

EVEN as late as 1919, statesmen would have accepted the ascendancy of Europe in the world as self-evident. If challenged, they could have demonstrated it from the events of the previous three centuries. Besides, as far as the world was concerned, Europe owned so much of it. In the arts, dominated within by the ideas of classical Greece, Europe showed only superiority to the rest of the globe. Oriental art was accepted where it was ornamental, symmetrical, or moral; any art that was grotesque or primitive was rejected.

Politically such a situation has been smashed beyond recognition. One has only to think of the Afro-Asian states, former European colonies, now active at U.N.O., to say nothing of all the factors—social, political, economic—which are helping to make the reality of one world. Has the situation, however, changed in cultural terms? Has Europe become open to other conventions? Has a true dialogue become possible?

I. THE WEST EXPOSED TO THE WORLD

The word 'Europe' itself presents a problem. The popular term 'The West' makes it clear that the U.S.A. is included, but suggests that Russia is not, which, of course, is wrong. In fact, one is largely thinking of the advanced industrial societies, which are easier to define by looking backwards. By 'Europe' or 'The West' one means those countries whose indigenous culture, however much rejected today, is Hellenic-Christian-Hebraic thought and belief. This is still unsatisfactory, but serves as a working guide.

95

(i) *A Shot-In-The-Arm from the Orient*

Spengler's *Decline of the West* underlined a motive for turning East for inspiration. If the West was run down, perhaps India or Japan or China, with their civilizations, thousands of years old, might offer wisdom and renewal. Certainly a number of Western artists have turned not only to the art but also to the religions of the 'Glorious East'.

India, for instance, fascinated Yeats. He knew the *Upanishads*, and some of his reflections on ideas of incarnation and the soul's rebirth appear in *A Vision*. He also wrote an enthusiastic introduction to Tagore's *Gitanjali*:

> 'I have carried the manuscript of these translations about with me for days, reading it in railway trains, or on the top of omnibuses and in restaurants, and I have often had to close it lest some stranger would see how much it moved me.'[1]

Aldous Huxley and Christopher Isherwood have drawn heavily on Indian religions for their own private beliefs. L. H. Myers set his philosophic novel *The Root and the Flower* in the India of Akbar. T. S. Eliot had more than an amateur knowledge of the *Bhagavad Gita*:

> ' "... Fare forward.
> O voyagers, O seamen,
> You who come to port, and you whose bodies
> Will suffer the trial and judgement of the sea,
> Or whatever event, this is your real destination."
> So Krishna, as when he admonished Arjuna
> On the field of battle.
> Not fare well,
> But fare forward, voyagers.'[2]

More essentially popular—not least through the writings of Pearl Buck and Lin Yutang—has been the thought world of China. Eisenstein studied Chinese ideas of audio-visual relationships:

> 'They derive from the principles of Yang and Yin, upon which is based the entire system of Chinese world-outlook and philosophy ... Yang and Yin—depicted as a circle, locked together within it *yang* and *yin*—*yang*, light; *yin*, dark—each

1. HENRY MOORE: *Reclining Figure* (1942)

There is no substitute for seeing Henry Moore's work, as it were, in the flesh. Although he has made a number of bronze castings, he has generally preferred to work directly in wood or stone, and allow his forms to be influenced by the distinctive nature and texture of the material under his hands. He has, however, also produced an important number of coloured drawings among the most famous of which are his wartime studies of miners and sleepers in air-raid shelters. This detail comes from one entitled *Red Rocks and Reclining Figure*. The rocks were two vivid red megaliths, hinting at the giant stones of the Avebury Circle, and with the strong suggestion that one might fit into the other.

2. SIDNEY NOLAN: *Ned Kelly*

Here is the outlaw in his self-made armour mask. He is an 'outsider' figure in conflict with society, but perhaps more at home in the apparent 'waste land' of the Australian out-back than in urban surroundings.

This picture is a detail from the second painting of the 27 Ned Kelly pictures by Nolan. They are painted in ripolin on hardboard and have a uniform size of 36 in. by 48 in. The originals are in vivid colour, not least in the ranges of orange, yellow and sepia of the harsh desert landscape.

The mask has been potent in modern art. From sources as diverse as those of African religions and Oriental drama, its influence can be seen as widely as Brecht's *Caucasian Chalk Circle*, Stravinsky's opera *Oedipus Rex* and Moore's helmet figures.

3. THE NEW CITY OF BRASILIA. 1956

Lucio Costa's bold,concept of the ground-plan was in the form of a
giant air-liner or cross (see page 107). The city itself is magnificently
sited at a river confluence.

The Congress Building (above) was designed, as were all the
buildings, by Oscar Niemeyer, and is in The Plaza of the Three
Towers. The giant statue is *The Pioneers* by Bruno Giorgi. The
famous Palace of the Dawn is in a commanding position overlooking
the main river. All three artists are themselves Brazilians.

4. **PABLO PICASSO**: a detail from *Guernica* (1937)

This famous picture was painted as an impassioned protest by Picasso against the obliteration bombing by German planes of the small town of Guernica during the Spanish Civil War. It was first displayed in the Spanish Pavilion at the Paris Exhibition 1937. Picasso made a large number of studies, experimenting to give his picture the maximum shock effect, but the basic content was clear in his mind from the start; the mangled body; the lamenting mother; the wounded bull and horse.

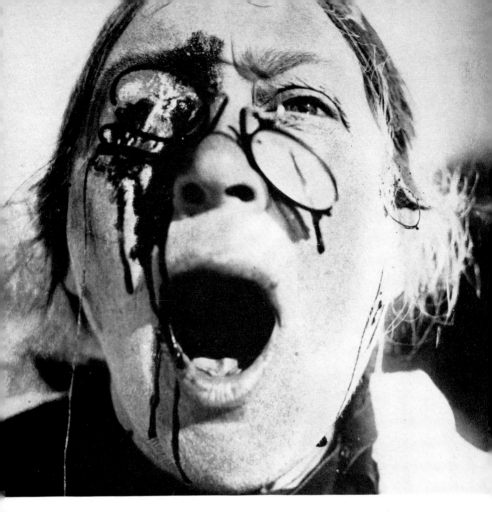

5. SERGE EISENSTEIN: *The Battleship Potemkin* (1925)

When the sailors mutiny the citizens of Odessa crowd the waterfront in their support, until they are brutally dispersed by Czarist troops. In the film the soldiers steadily descend a long flight of steps with fixed bayonets, driving every one before them. Eisenstein makes this an unforgettable sequence of striking and painful details; the run-away pram; the crumbling legs of the wounded man; and the gouged face of this elderly lady.

In its original version it was a silent film, and one of the many produced at the time for showing all over Russia to educate a partly illiterate peasantry in the ideology of Communism.

A similar still to this one probably gave Francis Bacon the idea for his Screaming Pope.

6. AKIRA KUROSAWA: *Rashomon* (1951)

A warrior is found killed in a wood. The film recounts, in a series of vivid flash-backs, how four different people claim that he met his death; a bandit, the ghost of the dead man himself, his wife and a peasant. The accounts are disturbingly different, and the truth remains ambiguous, even mysterious. The bandit had fled from the spot but had been wounded by an arrow (above). This had enabled him to be caught and taken for questioning.

Rashomon was probably the first Japanese film to win European acclaim after the end of the Second World War, and gained the Grand Prix in Venice in 1951. Kurosawa has used both contemporary and historical settings: outstanding among the latter are *Throne of Blood*—a version of *Macbeth*—and *The Seven Samurai*—honoured by a Hollywood copy.

7. **BERTOLT BRECHT**: *Mother Courage*

At the end Mother Courage has lost her two sons and her deaf daughter. She can only survive by pulling her cart herself and going on selling her wares to whichever warring soldiers will buy. War has destroyed her family but it will continue to be her livelihood. As she goes she sings the same cynical song as when one first met her, with its mocking echoes of a Bach chorale;

'Spring comes! Christian, awake!
The snow melts. The dead rest.
And what's not yet dead
Will now take to its heels.'

The actress here is Helene Weigel, Brecht's wife, in the production by the Berliner Ensemble.

8. SATYAJIT RAY: *Pather Panchali* (first film of the Apu trilogy 1954–1959)

Some account of these films will be found on page 106. Ray makes consistently vivid use of the human face—fresh, wrinkled, eager or resigned—throughout the whole trilogy. Ray was stimulated to make films by watching Jean Renoir making the film *The River* in Calcutta. He may have been influenced by Donskoi's *Maxim Gorky Trilogy* (1938–40) to which his own work is sometimes compared.

9. SUZANNE WENGER: *The Imprisonment of Obtala*

Obtala is the Yoruba (Nigerian) Creator-God. On one occasion, the belief is, he went to visit his friend, Shango, the God of thunder. On his journey he caught a runaway horse but was thrown into prison by Shango's servants as a thief. Shango, alas, only discovered who had been imprisoned after his country had suffered seven years of famine and distress.

This detail shows Obtala leaning down over the ritual play enacting his capture. Below him is the disc of the sun. The hands and mouth of one of Shango's servants can be seen in the bottom right, together with a lizard slipping away. There is another small figure by the God's mouth.

Suzanne Wenger, an Austrian artist, has lived for a number of years with the Yoruba people, and gained an exceptionally intimate knowledge of their art and religion. This picture is a large Batik, 9 ft. 6 in. by 14 ft., executed in the wax method in four colours: near black, pale yellowish-green, indigo, reddish brown.

10. MARTHA GRAHAM: *The Embattled Garden*

Traditionally the garden has been a symbol of happiness. Here, it would seem, the symbolism has darkened. The relationships have become more tortuous. The garden has become a prison or a defence position with hints of the enclosed room of Bacon's painting and Kafka's trapped individuals.

The Americans have been outstanding experimenters in the dance as an art form. They have taken an eclectic interest in the dance forms of the world. One of their vigorous sources has been American life itself in such examples as Agnes de Mille's *Rodeo*, Loring's *Billy the Kid*, Ruth Page's *Frankie and Johnny* and Jerome Robbins' dances for *West Side Story*.

Martha Graham has added her own *Appalachian Spring*. She says that she was moved by the vastness of unexplored America as a symbol of the unknown inner self. She has stressed that for her the dance is important both as a universal language and as a means of coming to understand one's true being. Both tasks may take a lifetime to learn. True to her belief she is still leading her company at the age of at least 65.

A number of modern composers have written music especially for her, including Milhaud, Hindemith and Aaron Copland.

11. LE CORBUSIER: HIGH COURT, CHANDIGARH (1951–56)

This is one of the most exciting buildings in the new capital city for the Punjab, which Le Corbusier planned in full for the government of India. A useful commentary on these purely 'upward-thrusting forces', the piers, is to see them in their full setting in Le Corbusier's perspective drawing above.

This also shows the giant statue of the *Open Hand* in the near distance, and the dramatic back-drop of the Himalayas.

12. ARNOLD SCHOENBERG: *Moses and Aaron*

This picture suggests the essential isolation of Moses, and his conflict
with Aaron. In Schoenberg's interpretation, Moses has solitary
experiences of the numinous, which he cannot adequately communicate. Unavoidably he must rely on Aaron to convey his unique
insights to the Jewish people.

This is a scene from the production at the Deutsche Oper, Berlin.

carrying within itself the essence of the other, each shaped to the other—*yang* and *yin*, forever opposed, forever united. An exceptionally pertinent principle for a film-maker to study.'[3]

Brecht had come to know Chinese poetry through the translations of Arthur Waley. In his exile he carried around with him, wherever he went, a hanging wall-roll depicting an ancient Chinese sage. Some of his poems reflect this influence, not least in their wry humour and sparse use of words. He also used China as a setting for three of his plays, of which *The Good Woman of Setzuan* is the best known. André Malraux, himself an expert on Oriental art, used Shanghai for the setting of *La Condition Humaine*.[4]

If the influence of India was largely in the realm of beliefs, China attracted the West for its urbanity of thought, its economy of means, and its sensitivity to the fine arts. The one, so to speak, offered content; the other, style. Japan offered something of both. Yeats and Brecht both studied the Japanese *Noh* play, and were attracted by its austerities. Benjamin Britten has used the same form successfully in his opera *Curlew River*. Zen Buddhism has been a helpful guide to Ionesco, in that it has offered him not an 'absurd', but an alternative logic to that of the West.

Yet when all is listed—and clearly the above are no more than jottings—doubts remain. The use made by any artist of such influences may be very unorthodox, and may not necessarily go very deep into his work. Brecht, for instance, welcomed the restraint of Chinese art, because it offered a curb to his own anarchy, but Setzuan might have been anywhere. As for Yeats, if he was interested in India, so was he also in Swedenborg, Celtic myth, the alchemists, Greece, Byzantium and theosophy. The final mix-up in *A Vision* remained essentially personal, and sustained few people but himself. Again, many artists have remained untouched by the Orient. Wherever is the influence of China on Picasso? Above all—and it is a problem to which we shall return—the main interest of western artists has been in the age-old art and beliefs of the East, at the very time when Eastern societies themselves were calling them seriously in question, finding them restrictive, or no longer valid in the twentieth century.

(ii) *Confrontation with the Foreign*

It is not that European man has suddenly seen Oriental scrolls, African masks or Aztec temples for the first time. He has seen them for hundreds of years. The point is that he has suddenly become able to look at them as though it were for the first time. André Malraux, in his splendid and beautifully illustrated *The Voices of Silence*, shows that it was not until western ideas of painting had broken down—the demand, for instance, for representation, and for Greek ideas of beauty—that we could genuinely see what was before our eyes:

'What our African explorers discovered was not Negro Art but fetishes, and what the conquistadors discovered was not Mexican art but Aztec idols. Similarly all the objects collected by Europeans on their island voyages passed for "curios". . . . Idols became works of art only when they were given a new frame of reference and could enter into an art world unknown to any civilization anterior to ours. Europe discovered Negro art when it could see African carvings in the context of Cézanne and Picasso—not as fetishes in an ambience of coconuts and crocodiles. It discovered great Chinese sculpture by way of Romanesque figures, not by way of the "chinoiseries" dear to our forefathers. . . . To begin with the metamorphosis of the past was a metamorphosis of our way of seeing; had there not been an aesthetic revolution, the sculpture of early periods, mosaics and stained glass would never have come to rank beside the painting of the Renaissance and the age of the great monarchs. Never would our ethnographical collections . . . have crossed the barrier between them and the art museums. Europe's dominion of the world would have served no purpose if it had not called forth the painting which removed the cataract from our western eyes and revealed for the first time the "formal dynamism" of works of art whose distortions had formerly been put down to ignorance or clumsiness. True modern art is not enough to account for these discoveries, but by subordinating appearance to creative vision, it has given access to a world in which a Mexican god becomes a statue and not a mere fetish, and Chardin's still-lifes join the Chartres Kings and the gods at Elephanta on a footing of equality: the first world of a truly "universal" art.'

More, however, was involved than a new way of seeing. For one thing, there was the sheer availability of art already mentioned—the photos, visits, reproductions forming what Malraux calls 'a museum without walls'. Again there has been a ground-swell of interest, springing from a sense of need:

> 'People of all lands, hardly aware of what they have in common, seem to be asking of the art of all time to fill a void they dimly sense within them.'

Lastly, there has been the breakdown of the limiting idea of progress:

> 'Chartres does not make an "advance" on Angkor, or Boro-budur, or the Aztec temples, any more than its Kings are an "advance" on the Kwannon at Nara, on the Plumed Serpents, or on Phidias' Horsemen. All are, for the first time, united in a world in which the dying fetishes are given a new lease of life such as they never knew before; in a world, where, also for the first time in history, Time is vanquished by the images that human hands created to defy it.'

The importance of all this is very great:

> 'It is in terms of a world-wide order that we are sorting out, tentatively as yet, the successive resuscitations of the whole world's past that are filling the first Museum without Walls . . . (We are) the first culture to include the whole world's art.'[5]

One strand of this story needs more attention—western man's excitement at his first clear gaze at the primitive. One artist who fully realizes his debt to primitive art is Henry Moore. 'All art', he said, 'has its roots in the primitive.' Primitive art is 'made by a people with a direct and immediate response to life'; it is 'a channel for expressing powerful beliefs, hopes and fears'.

Commenting on Negro art, he said:

> 'One of the first principles of art so clearly seen in primitive work is truth to material; the artist shows an instinctive understanding of his material, its right use and possibilities. Wood has a stringy fibrous consistency and can be carved into thin forms without breaking, and the Negro sculptor was able to free arms from the body, to have a space between the legs, and

to give his figures long necks when he wished. . . . For the Negro, as for other primitive peoples, sex and religion were the two interacting springs of life. Much Negro carving, like modern Negro spirituals but without their sentimentality, has pathos, a static patience and resignation to unknown mysterious powers; it is religious and, in movement, upward and vertical like the tree it was made from, but in its heavy bent legs is rooted in the earth. . . .'

Having looked too at Mexican and Oceanic art, he continues:

'Underlying these individual characteristics . . . a common world-language of form is apparent in them all: through the working of instinctive sculptural sensibility, the same shapes and form relationships are used to express similar ideas at widely different places and periods in history, so that the same form-vision may be seen in a Negro and a Viking carving, a Cycladic stone figure and a Nukuoro wooden statuette. . . .'[6]

Of course this excitement with the primitive goes further than the visual arts, and more people have joined in it than the artists themselves. Indeed it is an area where the artist can be greatly helped by the social scientists—anthropologists and psychologists. Many of the explorations into primitive societies are already proving fruitful, not least in showing how artistic creativity relates to the life of a group, to its communal activities and to its patterns of belief. Some of the play-back can be seen in the experimental work of American dance-groups, such as those of Martha Graham and Katherine Dunham.

An increasing interest is being shown in the poetry of Africa, and one result has been to spotlight qualities which western literature has neglected.

'The word here', said Senghor, 'is more than the image; it is the *analogous* image, without even the help of metaphor or comparison. It is enough to name the thing and the sense appears beneath the sign.'[7]

It has been pointed out that 'this process is essentially one of verbal magic; the poet-magus *makes* by naming'.[8] At one level, this has always been the force of poetry, and Europeans have been wrong in reducing 'magic' to the cliché of the 'pleasing' or 'heightened'. Such a mistake has, until recently, been less likely for Africans, because poetry was not something read alone quietly from a book, but something spoken aloud or sung in communities which still retained their rituals and dances. In such a situation, the very speaking of a name may be regarded as establishing a relationship:

> 'And I repeated your name: DYALLO!
> And you repeated my name: SENGHOR!'

'The word is active and creative; the master of language is the master of things.' And as the word still retains its primal power; it is a defence in face of uncertainties and mysteries:

> 'You in the unfairness of your justice have given me the
>   power of speech.
> Lord, harken to my voice. LET IT RAIN. It rains.
> And you have opened from your arms of thunder the
>   cataracts of forgiveness.'[9]

This whole area of language is likely to be a particularly fruitful subject of study. Among recent work, for instance, the anthropologist Lévi-Strauss has shown that all cultural phenomena —even *The Raw and the Cooked*, the title of his latest work—are a form of language. He has a special interest in two forms of language; the myth and music. 'Myths', he insists, 'are translations of one another, and the only way you can understand a myth is to show how a translation is offered by a different myth.' For him, 'music (is) the only language, both untranslatable and immediately understandable' and is the 'supreme mystery of the science of man, the mystery against which science must necessarily butt its head'. 'The creator of music' is 'a being similar to the gods'.[10]

Orpheus will return later. It has been useful, if over-simple, to see the re-discovery of the primitive—within himself, and externally in the world—as one of the sources of a new vitality. The real difficulty is that for non-western man, particularly the African, this is the very thing he wants to escape from. He is interested in modernity, not in the archaic, and he sees no task as more urgent than bringing his country smart and with-it into the industrial world of the twentieth century.

2. THE WORLD'S APPROACH TO THE WEST

The rest of the world may look at the west with bitterness, but it cannot avoid its way of life, for it contains its own future. Hence all the turmoil of long-term loans, technical experts, western-trained students, U.N. assistance. Such things may help to bring the developing areas into the industrial twentieth century, but they cannot be the methods of the arts. To put themselves sharp and alive on the cultural map of the modern world requires other approaches, and raises its own difficulties.

(i) *To Out-west the West, or Over-act Themselves*

The movement for women's rights found itself considering two aims: to out-man the man or to be self-consciously feminine. Translated, these provide two possible routes for non-western peoples facing western culture: either they become more contemporary than New York and more *avant-garde* than Paris, or they dig in and assert their own indigenous product. Both ways have been tried—at times side by side—and neither are wholly satisfying answers.

To go western was confusing. It was difficult for many countries to get round a central fact: they had only recently (or perhaps not yet) ceased to be colonies of European powers. Leaving aside Latin America, whose colonial experience was long distant, large areas of Africa and Asia faced the dilemma: to go western appeared like following old masters, yet one of the key weapons, anyway for writers, if they wished to reach more than a parochial audience was the language learnt in colonial schools—probably French or English. The real difficulty lay deeper, and was not political but artistic: namely, the problem of being creative in a second language with no deep roots in native culture.

Surprisingly, instead of stressing the difficulty, the story is one of success. To consider only novels, and ones written in English, there are:

Peter Abrahams: *A Wreath for Udomo*; V. S. Naipaul: *A House for Mr. Biswas* (West Indies); Amos Tutuola: *The Palm-Wine Drinkard*; Chinua Achebe: *Things Fall Apart*; Wole Soyinke: *The Interpreters* (Nigeria); James Ngugi: *The River Between* (Kenya); R. K. Narayan: *The Man-Eater of Malgudi* (India).

This is just a handful of books, chosen at random, not to assess their literary merit, but to point to their extraordinary vitality and variety. By any standards, these add to the life of literature by giving something direct from their own backgrounds.

This search for one's own identity is involved in language, but also has other roots. It has been suggested that the real conflict is not between the use of the vernacular and the use of French or English. For one thing the choice was not open: 'I have been given this language,' said Chinua Achebe, 'and I intend to use it.' The real decision may be between facing towards the past or towards the present; and for some it is not a problem of choice but of how to live holding both in consciousness. The following poem by the Ghanaian poet George Awooner-Williams was quoted in an article in *The Times Literary Supplement*.

> My god of songs was ill
> And I was taking him to be cured . . .
> I gathered courage
> I knocked on the fetish hut
> And the cure god said in my tongue
> 'Come in with your backside'
> With my god of songs crying on my head. . . .
> The cure god said I had violated my god
> 'Take him to your father's gods' he said in my tongue
> So I took him to my father's gods
> But before they opened the hut
> My god burst into songs, new strong songs
> That I am still singing with him.

And the writer commented:

'Note that the cure god speaks always "in my tongue". Yet the poem itself is written in English, and perhaps this expresses the kind of balance between world language and vernacular at which writers of large vision will aim. The vernacular for what is local and inmost, what ties one to a special piece of earth; the world language for retailing the message to the world. It is as if a man might sit in his house and speak to his god in his own tongue, then turn and speak to us in English. If he becomes too intent on translating everything for us, he may injure his vision and his art; but if he becomes wholly absorbed in talking with his god, his audience must remain a tribal one.'[11]

It is against this background—vernacular v. world language; past v. present—that one can consider *Négritude*. Started among others by the Martiniquan Aimé Césaire and the Senegalese poet-statesman Léopold Senghor it attempted to explore and proclaim the essence of being Negro, whether in Africa or America. Hailed by Sartre as the 'sole great revolutionary poetry' and by Breton as 'rien moins que le plus grand monument lyrique de ce temps', after a bare ten years, its prestige is already on the wane. It is not that it produced bad verse, indeed much is moving and powerful:

> 'ma négritude n'est pas une pierre, sa surdité ruée
> contre la clameur du jour
> ma négritude n'est pas une taie d'eau morte sur
> l'oeil mort de la terre
> ma négritude n'est ni une tour ni une cathédrale
> elle plonge dans la chair rouge du sol
> elle plonge dans la chair ardente du ciel
> elle troue l'accablement opaque de sa droite patience . . .'

The problem is rather that it seemed, especially to the English-speaking African, to be a hot-house product from Paris, providing the kind of primitivism that the West lapped up, and being negative to industrialism. This is not to condemn it: it is only to show the extreme difficulty of discovering one's identity over against the European world.[12]

This search for identity was a real one, too, in countries which already had a strong literary tradition and had not been colonies of western powers. Here the need was to reform themselves—their language and art conventions—before they could successfully and without false imitation benefit from western experiment and new ideas. Such is the story of China since the Revolution of 1911. In the same year as the Russian Revolution, Hu Shih, in discussing the reform of Chinese literature, suggested 'Eight Don'ts', including 'Don't use classical allusions'; 'Don't purposely avoid slang'; 'Don't imitate ancient literature'. These suggestions were elaborated by Chen Tu-hsiu in the next issue of the magazine *La Jeunesse* into a three-point programme for reform:

> '1. Doing away with the ornate and obsequious literature of the aristocratic few and creating a simple and lyrical literature of the people.

'2. Doing away with the cliché-ridden and grandiose literature of classicism and creating a fresh and honest literature of realism.

'3. Doing away with a pedantic and obscure literature of escapism and creating a plain-speaking and popular literature of society in general.'[13]

All this amounted to a literary revolution. The movement was supported by an influential group of professors from Peking University, and in 1919 merged with the politically-idealistic May Fourth Student Movement. Moreover their work was complemented by the attempts of the Ministry of Education to romanize the script, standardize pronunciation, and to make the vernacular compulsory for the first two years of the primary school. One of the most successful authors of these years, Lu Hsun, best known for his *A Madman's Diary*, showed it was possible to be exposed to European ideas and remain truly Chinese. Among his epigrams, the most pertinent here ran:

'Who says that the Chinese do not change? When new things are introduced they want to reject them, but when they begin to see that there is something in them they begin to change. But they do not change by adapting themselves to new things, but by adapting the new things to themselves.'[14]

It would be interesting to explore how far this is still true under communist China. The underlying questioning, however, about one's national identity is very symptomatic of the modern world.

(ii) *The Quivering Needle*

'When you are spiritually emancipated, the needle quivers around the central point—the meeting point between rejection and acceptance. Then you know both how excruciating and exciting it is to be the meeting point of two streams of consciousness and the paradoxes they pose. That is what makes our art.'[15]

The difficulties touched on in the last section are very real and will be for many years to come. Yet exciting art has emerged where men have accepted the tension of honouring opposed traditions. Fruitful examples come from India, Brazil and Africa.

From India the West has been enriched by the films of Satyajit

Ray. He has been able to use with great skill (and often in very frustrating circumstances) the most technological and twentieth-century of mediums but with a close feeling for people. He insists that 'there is nothing more important in a film than the emotional integrity of the relationships it depicts'.[16] His outstanding achievement is probably his Apu trilogy: *Pather Panchali*; *Aparajito*; *The World of Apu*, a family saga focused on Apu, from child to man. One might think of them as films where two worlds cross: those of the river and the railway. One is never far from rivers, and the sequence of life from birth to death. One is never far from the railway, which passes by the isolated, almost unbelievably poor village on its way to the modern city. Both worlds meet in Apu, and in his experience of tragedy: the death of his little sister after they had been caught in a tropical downpour and there was no medical help for her fever; the leaving of his wrinkled old grandmother to starve to death because food was desperately short; the early death of his father, 'a harried clerk who would rather be a poet', who had mistakenly brought his family to live in the city; the death of his young wife in childbirth. Yet what stays in the mind is not misery, but a disturbing beauty: the sense of childhood as Apu and his sister rush through a field of flowers to watch the train; the power of faces—shy, sad, laughing, angry; the stubborn warmth of his mother; the final reconciliation with his own young son. Here is both a record of an Indian village and of universal experience.

From India also comes a fruitful meeting of another kind: a western artist being invited to answer a local need. In this case Le Corbusier was asked to design the new capital city of the Punjab at Chandigarh. Bringing with him the technical know-how of the West, he used both that and his own rich inventiveness to evolve a new city that seemed an exciting but inevitable growth out of the local tradition and the geographical setting: twentieth-century vitality against the backdrop of the Himalayas. The city was planned in 30 rectangular sectors. Each sector has an area of 250 acres, a housing capacity of 15,000, and is self-contained in civic amenities. Different parts of the city are devoted to specific functions—government, the university, industry—the latter being separated from the rest by a 400 ft. green belt, just as fast-moving traffic is separated from the traffic of the sectors. For the arts, the focus of interest is doubtless in the design of individual buildings—especially in that for the High Court. As an American architect has said, the High Court:

'. . . enforces the view towards the mountains, and the horizontal roof line of the strict envelope in which it is contained carries the eye towards them, indicating once more the real boundaries of the space. Within this frame the High Court is a great, hollowed-out, concrete mass. Its glass skin is again masked, on the entrance side, by a *brise-soleil* which keeps the scale integral and pushes upward and out with threatening power. Up through this projection, continued further upward by the hung vaults of the canopy, rise the great piers as purely upward-thrusting forces. Between these, men enter, and ramps of an almost Piranesian violence rise behind them. . . . Le Corbusier's (piers) aggrandize the man who stands before them by stretching his own force empathetically upward with them. In this way, in balance with the landscape forms, they embody the human act of authority in the court.

'Men thus return to the earth as men. . . . They appear to reject protection and mobility alike—so leave the cave, come off the road, forsake the river, and take a stand. This seems the fullest realization in architecture so far of the new humanity, self-governing and expecting no favours . . . "a shaft . . . inflexible and free".'[17]

In the same decade—the nineteen-fifties—Brazil also started building a new capital. Once again scientific expertise and artistic imagination worked together, with the team-work characteristic of success in modern architecture. The greatest care was taken over the site: a commission investigated all the essential points—climate; drainage; geology; land use; engineering; transport; scenery; building materials, and so on. The basic plan of this—'the world's first air-age capital'—resembled a huge air-liner or cross, explained by the designer, Lucio Costa, as the primary gesture of one who marks or takes possession of a place. One of the most pleasing buildings is the president's house—the Palace of the Dawn—designed by the Brazilian architect, Oscar Niemeyer; one of the most exciting is the Congress building with its columns of rooms leaping to the sky, and the wide open space in front, focused by the giant statuary of *The Pioneers* by Bruno Giorgi. Yet, alas, this exhilarating city of the space-age is already cursed with its slum-area, and 'typifies the exploding social situation characteristic of much of Latin America'.[18]

Such an exploding situation and its consequences would be familiar to an African, and add yet another level to his experience. Many parts of Africa, too, have another vital element in their experience: that of multi-racialism. The more the world itself becomes one society, the more it will know the pressures, difficulties and opportunities of multi-racial living. This fact means that much modern African art, despite all the present perplexities to its creators touched on in the last section, has a peculiar significance and value for the future. Ezekiel Mphahlele—quoted at the start—is well aware that multi-racialism must be embraced: 'I personally cannot think of the future of my people in South Africa as something in which the white man does not feature.' And again, 'The pain of not being nationalists lies in the cold realism of it. We are aiming at a common society and to prove that multi-racial societies can thrive and become a glorious reality in Africa.' He insists that this will place a special demand on the creative arts:

'If the autonomy of art means anything at all, it is that art should order our experiences and responses and help resolve conflicts inside ourselves as individuals in such a way that we each bring to our groups a personality that could never justify race, colour, and religious discrimination, intellectual dishonesty, poverty and inequality of privilege!'

Against this background, one can point to the value of such a deeply-felt novel as Chinua Achebe's *Things Fall Apart*, aptly borrowing a phrase from Yeats. The story tells of the catastrophic impact on an African village of the arrival of the white man at the end of the last century. 'The clash portrayed by Achebe', wrote Mphahlele, 'has a symbolic significance for all Africa. It is a symbol of that larger irony which is the meeting point between reconciliation and conflict; it has, therefore, important reference to the larger context of black-white contact.'[19] Inevitably its truth contains pain. The hero, the warrior Okonkwo, at the climax of the story commits suicide. One feels that such a conclusion is not only psychologically correct for this harsh man who hated 'everything that his father Unoka had loved. One of these things was gentleness and another was idleness.' Such a death also symbolized the abrupt ending of a way of life.

'That night the Mother of the Spirits walked the length and breadth of the clan, weeping for her murdered son. It was a terrible night. Not even the oldest man in Umuofia had ever heard such a strange and fearful sound, and it was never to be heard again. It seemed as if the very soul of the tribe wept for a great evil that was coming—its own death.'[20]

REFERENCES

1. YEATS, W. B.: From the introduction to TAGORE, R.: *Gitanjali* (Song Offerings) (Macmillan, 1913).*
2. ELIOT, T. S.: *Four Quartets*, op. cit. From 'The Dry Salvages'.
3. EISENSTEIN, S. M.: *The Film Sense*, op. cit., p. 79.
4. MALRAUX, A.: *La Condition Humaine*. Translated as *Man's Estate* (in U.S. *Man's Fate*) by A. MacDonald (Methuen, 1948.)*
5. MALRAUX, A.: *The Metamorphosis of the Gods* (Secker), pp. 20–1, 34–5, and *The Voices of Silence*, op. cit., pp. 127, 640.
6. MOORE, H.: *Henry Moore on Sculpture*, op cit. From his broadcast 'Primitive Art', pp. 155, 159. This lavish book gives illustrations not only of Moore's work, but also of the primitive sculptures he refers to.
7. SENGHOR, LÉOPOLD SÉDAR: *Ethiopiques* (Seuil, 1956), p. 108.
8. MOORE and BEIER (eds.): *Modern Poetry from Africa* (Penguin African Library). From the Introduction, pp. 26–7.
9. REED, J. and WAKE, C. (eds.): *Selected Poems of Léopold Sédar Senghor* (O.U.P., 1964). From Introduction, p. xviii; and p. 94. The two Senghor quotations are from his poems 'Mediterranean' and 'The Elegy of the Waters'.
10. LÉVI-STRAUSS, C.: See STEINER, G.: 'A Conversation with Claude Lévi-Strauss' in *Encounter*, April 1966, Vol. XXVI, No. 4, pp. 37–8. A list of Lévi-Strauss's works in translation is given on p. 33.
11. AWOONER-WILLIAMS, G.: Three of his poems are included in the Moore and Beier anthology, op. cit., pp. 78–81. The essay appeared in the special number of *The Times Literary Supplement* devoted to Commonwealth writing (September 16, 1965), with the title 'Finding Their Voices', pp. 791–2.
    See also REED, J., and WAKE, C.: *Book of African Verse* (African Writers. Heinemann Educational Books, 1964).

12. See same number of *The Times Literary Supplement* for the essay *Twilight of a Dark Myth* from which the quotations in French are taken, pp. 805–6.

13. CHEN TU-HSIU: Quoted from LAI MING: *A History of Chinese Literature* (Cassell, 1964), pp. 346–56: 'The Literary Revolution'. (See also BARRACLOUGH, G.: *An Introduction to Contemporary History* (Watts, 1964. New Thinkers Library, Chapter VIII).)*

14. LU HSUN: ibid., p. 372.

15. MPHAHLELE, E.: *The African Image* (Faber, 1964), p. 53.*

16. RAY, S.: From an article in *Sequence*. Quoted from HOUSTON, P.: *The Contemporary Cinema* (Penguin, 1963), p. 53. A full discussion of Ray's work can be found in BARNOUW, E., & KRISHNASWAMY, S.: *Indian Film* (Columbia University Press, 1963).

17. SCULLY, V., Jr.: *Modern Architecture—The Architecture of Democracy* (Readers Union; Prentice-Hall International, London, 1964), p. 48.

18. See BLAKEMORE, H.: *Latin America* (The Modern World Series. O.U.P. 1966).*

19. MPHAHLELE, E.: op. cit., pp. 66, 74, 94, 202.

20. ACHEBE, C.: *Things Fall Apart* (Heinemann Educational Books, 1962, African Writers Series), pp. 13, 168.

CHAPTER FOUR

The Primal Ground

AN interest in world art cannot avoid a look at religion as one of the sources of art, for the great religions have claimed to be of universal validity. Such a claim has been challenged sharply in this century, and almost all the religious systems of the world have undergone scrutiny, and a weakening of popular appeal. Under such an attack, some of the basic features of religion have been called in question—the framework of theology and myth, the belief in a transcendent Being, the trust in a God involved in this world, the validity of worship.

The second part of this book will pursue such issues more fully. What matters here is the repercussion of this process on art. Giving the broadest meaning to the words religion and art it is possible to regard them as inseparable: the ground of art is a living religion, and the richest nourishers of religion are the creative arts.

I. TO HELL AND BACK—THE MYTHIC SEARCH

A religion, then, may be expected to have its framework of theology and myth, where the myth may be thought of as the world-view in symbolic, story form. As such, the myth is apprehendable by the whole community, and will continuously fructify in the individual's consciousness, giving him a 'sense of relationship between the rim of private experience and the hub of the great wheel of being'.[1] At least it will if the myth is sustained by the imagination and work of the poet, musician and painter, whether they use the myth precisely as Dante or implicitly as Shakespeare used Christian myth. In doing so, the artists are not just acting as

publicity men for the faith, for they gain for their work a significant frame, which has both internal coherence and an aura of
meaning beyond itself.

Faced with the breakdown of the central myth of Christianity,
modern artists have made a number of makeshift answers; 'makeshift' in that none has shown itself indisputably successful. One
approach was to attempt, as Claudel and Eliot have done, to
shore up the broken myth. Another was to return and re-use
Greek myth, such as Sartre and Cocteau have done. A third
possibility was, if one believed in it, as Brecht did, to use modern
Marxism; for with its dynamic story of class revolution it has
both the power and the comprehensiveness to qualify as a myth,
backed too by a theoretic defence. An outstanding survey of all
these approaches can be found in Steiner's *The Death of Tragedy*.

At least one thing becomes clear in these struggles of modern
writers—the value of a framework provided by a myth. Interesting
examples here are those near contemporaries—Joyce's *Ulysses*
and Eliot's 'Waste Land'. Faced with the amorphous mass of
material which constitutes Leopold Bloom's experience in one
day in Dublin added to Joyce's own scattered interests in language,
art and thought, then the Ulysses myth was a godsend, less to
provide meaning than an organizing idea. All of this Eliot appre-
ciated in his review of the book:

> 'I hold this book to be the most important expression which
> the present age has found. . . . In using the myth, in manipula-
> ing a continuous parallel between contemporaneity and an-
> tiquity Mr. Joyce is pursuing a method which others must
> pursue after him. They will not be imitators, any more than
> the scientist who uses the discoveries of an Einstein in pursuing
> his own, independent, further investigations. It is simply a way
> of controlling, of ordering, of giving a shape and significance
> to the immense panorama of futility and anarchy which is
> contemporary history.'[2]

Eliot's description would also apply to his own work, for he had
taken the myths of the fertility rituals as the organizing idea behind 'The Waste Land'. Drawn, as he freely admits, from Jesse
Weston's *From Ritual to Romance*, this body of myths represented
both archaic elements, earlier than classical Greece, and also the
themes which had become Christianized in the Grail story, thus

drawing together two basic sources of western civilization. Yet Eliot's success remains in doubt, and at the end of the poem all he can offer are 'fragments I have shored against my ruins'.

If the attempt to use a given body of myth might seem to have failed, another course of action was probably even more vulnerable, namely to attempt to create one's own framework of myth. Lawrence, 'worshipping the dark gods and the fire in the blood', Yeats with his bizarre cycle, explained by word and diagram in *A Vision*, Rilke and his angels, to say nothing of the strange beasts and figures of the visual artists, have all attempted this. 'But,' comments Steiner:

> 'where an artist must be the architect of his own mythology, time is against him. He cannot live long enough to impose his special vision and the symbols which he has devised for it on the habits of language and feeling in his society. . . . The idiosyncratic world image, without an orthodox or public frame to support it, is kept in focus only by virtue of the poet's present talent. It does not take root in the common soil. . . . The mythologies that have centred the imaginative habits and practices of western civilization, that have organized the inner landscape were not the product of individual genius. A mythology crystallizes sediments accumulated over great stretches of time. It gathers into conventional form the primal memories and historical experiences of the race. Being the speech of the mind when it is in a state of wonder or perception, the great myths are elaborated as slowly as is language itself.'[3]

This stultified mythic search has meant stresses and strains for both artist and audience. For the audience, because excessive demands may have been put on their understanding. If a myth is not based on a known 'theology', then the reader must make an extreme effort to become familiar with that artist's private world, or alternatively, an almost unbearable amount of explanation is left to the critic. For the artist, because his search for a myth—for a 'centre which implies a circumference'—will be a solitary one. Writing of such men as Rilke and Lawrence, Spender said:

> 'What all these have in common is the centre of isolated creative individuality: the idea that the individual in his own

solitude, accepting the modern environment as the "destructive element" in which he is immersed, can create out of that solitude an "answer".'[4]

And there is the added difficulty that ours is an age of prose, whereas poetry is the language of myth.

There is, however, a myth that would seem to be the myth of poetic power itself, namely Orpheus, and it is one that has appealed to several modern writers—Cocteau, for instance, Anouilh, Lawrence, and, above all, Rilke. Orpheus descended into the underworld to rescue Eurydice, just as in an analogous way modern artists have gone into darkness to rescue their creativity:

'Reach me a gentian, give me a torch
let me guide myself with the blue, forked torch of this flower
down the darker and darker stairs. . . .
to the sightless realm where darkness is awake upon the dark
and Persephone herself is but a voice
or a darkness invisible enfolded in the deeper dark. . . .'[5]

They have explored their own depths; the destructiveness of the contemporary world; neglected and archaic forms—'ghosts', as it were, of mankind's past. Such a journey may have restored a primal force to the music of their work, which can be transforming in its power:

'Choose to be changed. With the flame, with the flame be
    enraptured,
where from within you a thing changefully-splendid escapes.'

*

'Dead evermore is Eurydice, mount with more singing,
mount to relation more pure with more celebrant tongue.
Here, in this realm of the dwindlers and dregs, be a ringing
glass, which has, even though shivered to pieces, been rung.'

For such a journey may have exposed them to destruction—perhaps by frenzy or by hard denial:

'You that could sound till the end, though, immortal accorder,
seized by the scorn-maddened Maenads' intemperate throng,
wholly outsounded their cries when in musical order
soared from the swarm of deformers your formative song.

Wrestle and rage as they might on that fated career,
none was able to shatter your head or your lyre:
hard stones hurled at your heart could only acquire
gentleness, soon as they struck you, and power to hear.
Though they destroyed you at last and revenge had its will,
sound of you lingered in lions and rocks you were first to
enthral, in the trees and the birds. You are singing there still.

O you god that has vanished! You infinite track!
Only because dismembering hatred dispersed you
are we hearers today and a mouth which else Nature would
lack.'[6]

2. THE SUPERNATURAL—A DEVILISH INTRUSION

There is an uncanny sense of crucifixion in Orpheus' death, as
though a phantom orthodoxy had come in by the back door.
Strictly speaking, the super-natural is an essential element of
religious belief: the belief, that is, in a transcendent God, in a
being above and beyond the material world. But as this is a
belief—anyway in a popular sense—in a reality outside the realm
of science, God has dwindled and the supernatural has become
reduced to spooks.

If modern art has 'supped full of horrors', it has also been
haunted by ghosts. Ibsen's *Ghosts*, the man the children meet in
Henry James' *The Turn of the Screw*, *The Man Outside* of Wolf-
gang Borchert—the returning soldier, dead or not dead, in the
Elbe, Amos Tutuola's *My Life in the Bush of Ghosts*, all the
characters of Sartre's *Huis Clos*, the unseen presences in Ionesco's
The Chairs, the dead brother in Miller's *Death of a Salesman*, the
dead father in Kop's *The Hamlet of Stepney Green*, mysterious
orders in Pinter's *The Dumb Waiter*, the pursuers of *The Family
Reunion*, the boy who comes from Godot to Beckett's waiting
tramps. One has to stretch the meaning of the word to include
such a ghostly company. Who are they? Fears? Guilts repressed
and returning? Attitudes that refuse to die? Denials that refuse to
be denied and become unwanted intrusions? A questioning of
death? 'Intimations of Immortality'? Unintentionally, we are, it
seems, with Orpheus in Pluto's kingdom.

Or perhaps we are in the ruined chapel of 'The Waste Land'.
Certainly sudden reminders of ruined religious beliefs can appear
ghostly. The German artist Kurt Schwitters collected rubbish
and turned it into a structure called *a cathedral built with things*—
it took him ten years and 'three storeys of his house had to be
demolished to give him the space he needed'.[7] Jimmy Porter being
abusive about Alison's mother—'she will pass away, my friends,
leaving a trail of worms gasping for laxatives behind her—from
purgatives to purgatory', or against Helena—the 'sacred cow',
'apocalyptic share-pusher', going down 'to the ecstatic little shed
at the bottom of the garden to relieve her sense of guilt'[8]—all this
has more than a hint of Luther, and even his trumpeting is upset
by intruding church bells. Joyce's Dublin has these disturbing
echoes, even in a brothel:

> '. . . If the second advent came to Coney Island are we ready?
> Florry Christ, Stephen Christ, Zoe Christ, Bloom Christ, Kitty
> Christ, Lynch Christ, it's up to you to sense that cosmic force.
> Have we cold feet about the cosmos? No. Be on the side of the
> angels. Be a prism. You have that something within, the higher
> self. You can rub shoulders with a Jesus, a Gautama, an Inger-
> soll. Are you all in this vibration? . . .
> '. . . White yoghin of the Gods. Occult pimander of Hermes
> Trismegistos. (With a voice of whistling seawind.) Punarjanam
> patsypunjaub! I won't have my leg pulled. It has been said
> by one: beware the left, the cult of Shakti. (With a cry of storm-
> birds.) Shakti, Shiva! Dark hidden Father! (He smites with his
> bicycle pump the crayfish in his left hand. On its cooperative
> dial glow the twelve signs of the zodiac. . . .)'[9]

Here again is art made out of rubbish—the rubbish of world
beliefs—but it is not harmless rubbish.

What once had disturbed as blasphemy now disturbs in the way
that paintings of the Surrealists disturb, or those of Chirico already described. Paintings of still objects, apparently thrown
away, can be most menacing. It is partly the unexpected juxta-
positions—a classical bust, a surgical glove; it is partly the searchlight sharpness of outline and detail; but above all it is the ghostly
feeling that the objects are alive and hostile to man. Here one
touches the demonic strand in modern art. One meets it again in
the possessed figures from Dostoievsky, through Munch to Klee,

and on to the shrieking girls in Miller's *The Crucible* and the demented nuns in Whiting's *The Devils*. It is no wonder that modern artists have discovered the horror pictures of Bosch and Goya to complement their own creations.

Yet this intrusion of the demonic is balanced by an intrusion of the archaic and earthly—the satyrs and fauns of Picasso, already mentioned. A fine example of this comes in the long short-story of the Provençal writer D'Arbaud called *The Beast of the Vaccarés*. Set in the lonely wasteland at the delta of the Rhône, it tells of a dying satyr. The climax is a wild stampede of the herds.[10] Here is force and fecundity—the chthonic. It shows itself too in some of the interest in the primitive. In this context, material objects again have a special significance, not of menace but of vitality. 'Everything that is dead quivers. Not only the things of poetry, stars, moon, wood, flowers, but even a white trouser button glittering out of a puddle in the street. . . . Everything has a secret soul, which is silent more often than it speaks.'[11] For Rilke too, things mattered:

> '. . . Are we, perhaps, *here* just for saying: House,
> Bridge, Fountain, Gate, Jug, Fruit Tree, Window,—
> possibly: Pillar, Tower? . . . but for *saying*, remember,
> oh, for such saying as never the things themselves
> hoped so intensely to be.'[12]

It was a short step from here to a belief in inspiration for the artist as a kind of dionysiac force. Such a belief, as has been seen, is out of step with much contemporary taste, but was emphatically held by Rilke. He speaks of 'days of enormous obedience', of 'a storm of the spirit' which threatened to annihilate the body. 'O that I was allowed to survive to this day, throughout everything. Wonder. Grace.'[13] And it is only a change of image rather than of experience to the claim of Paul Klee:

> 'It is the artist's mission to penetrate as far as may be toward that secret ground where primal law feeds growth. Which artist would not wish to dwell at the central organ of all motion in space-time (be it the brain or the heart of creation) from which all functions derive their life? In the womb of nature, in the primal ground of creation, where the secret key to all things lies hidden?. . . . Our beating heart drives us downward, far down to the primal ground.'[14]

Another myth, and oddly another descent, may focus this intrusion of the chthonic: *Dr. Faustus* and the imagined descent of
its hero into the depths of the sea. The central figure of Mann's
novel is significantly enough himself an artist—a musician, whose
methods of serial composition were based on the ideas of Schoenberg. At one point, out of a kind of bizarre mischief, he invents the
story of a descent into the depths of the sea:

> 'After that, indeed long before the hand of the indicator
> stood at seven hundred and fifty to seven hundred and sixty-
> five metres, came solid blackness all round, the blackness of
> interstellar space whither for eternities no weakest sun-ray had
> penetrated, the eternally still and virgin night, which now had
> to put up with a powerful artificial light from the upper
> world. . . .
> '. . .Adrian spoke of the itch one felt to expose the unexposed,
> to look at the unlooked-at, the not-to-be and not-expecting-to-
> be-looked-at. There was a feeling of indiscretion, even of guilt,
> bound up with it, not quite allayed by the feeling that science
> must be allowed to press just as far forwards as it is given the
> intelligence of scientists to go. . . .
> '. . . Indescribable was everything that went whisking past the
> windows in a blur of motion: frantic caricatures of organic
> life; predatory mouths opening and shutting; obscene jaws,
> telescope eyes; the paper nautilus; silver- and gold-fish with
> goggling eyes on top of their heads; heteropods and pteropods,
> up to two or three yards long. Even those that floated passively
> in the flood, monsters compact of slime, yet with arms to catch
> their prey, polyps, acalephs, skyphmedusas—they all seemed
> to have been seized by spasms of twitching excitement. . . .'

So Adrian held forth on 'his experiences of the monstrously
extra-human', and in the end 'the Devil claimed his soul'.[15]

3. WHAT HAPPENED AFTER GOD DIED

One started to discuss the supernatural and discovered a very
heightened sense of the vitality of the material world.

> 'God, the no longer sayable, is being stripped of his attri-
> butes: they return to his creation.'[16]

This raises another key issue of religious belief, namely that of immanence, the belief that God is present and involved in his creation; that he is, in some sense, incarnate in it. Yet few remarks have had more sense of the *Zeitgeist*, have been more resonant for modern man, than Nietzsche's words 'God is dead'.

If God is dead, then the world is left without him, and it has become the Waste Land of the artists' imagination. As already suggested, there will be 'No Hero in a Landscape', because men are anxious, feeling themselves to be without guidance, without future, and alone. They are trapped like Dallapiccola's *Prisoner*, 'tortured with hope'. It is this underlying sense of catastrophe which gives such force to Kafka's *Castle*, which otherwise would seem only a banal story of bureaucratic caprice:

> 'Instead, (the authorities) let K. go anywhere he liked—of course, only within the village—and thus pampered and ener-vated him, ruled out all possibility of conflict, and transposed him to an unofficial, totally unrecognized, troubled and alien existence.'[17]

Here is the 'frontier situation' of the existentialist, explored by Heidegger and Jaspers, and popularized by Sartre. The individual is without maps, without orders, and must act in desperation. So much of this could be dismissed as metaphor, were it not that the actual experiences of twentieth-century man—in wars, camps, flight, exile—has been of just that terrible kind.

If modern man has had to go through horror, however, it is another consequence of God's death that the expression of such experience in the arts cannot have the dignity and assurance of tragedy. It has been possible for individuals, of course, to have what Unamuno explored—*The Tragic Sense of Life*—but not for dramatists dependent on a shared thought-world with their audience. Tragedy was possible when:

> '... the alphabet of tragic drama—such concepts as grace and damnation, purgation and relapse, innocence and corruption through demonic power—retained a clear and present meaning.'

> (For) 'tragedy is that form of art which requires the intoler-able burden of God's presence. It is now dead because His shadow no longer falls upon us as it fell on Agamemnon or Macbeth or Athalie.'[18]

Tragedy moves its audience because their frailty lies at the
heart of it, but if God is dead, then man must take his place and
be more than man—the Superman of Nietzsche's demand:

'He who no longer finds what is great in God will find it
nowhere—he must either deny it or create it.

'Indeed who can feel with me what it means to feel with
every shred of one's being that the weight of all things must be
defined anew.'[19]

So man must create and define, think and act, as if he were God.
One by-product of such an attitude for the arts is that creativity
comes to be worshipped as an end in itself. Art becomes a religion.

But man, of course, cannot be superman. He fails. He is
hurled into catastrophes of his own making. He re-discovers the
pain of the human condition:

'Only man can fall from God
Only man.

No animal, no beast nor creeping thing
no cobra nor hyena nor scorpion nor hideous white ant
can slip entirely through the fingers of the hands of god
into the abyss of self-knowledge,
knowledge of the self-apart-from-god.'[20]

Again, a figure may focus the theme: *Mother Courage*, isolated
in the waste land of Europe in the Thirty Years' War. She is
trapped in that situation. One first sees her with her cart, and
one's last view is of her struggling away with it. Her terrain is
the no-man's-land, the undefined frontier between warring armies.
She survives only by being totally amoral, selling her wares
indifferently to either side. By the finish, she has experienced the
unbearable catastrophe of losing her three children. Yet Brecht
did not want his audience to be moved, as with a tragedy, and
partly rewrote it after the first Zurich performance to try to
prevent this. Luckily, he failed. As George Steiner said:

'There comes a moment in *Mother Courage* when the soldiers
carry in the dead body of Schweizerkas. They suspect that he
is the son of Courage but are not quite certain. She must be
forced to identify him. I saw Helene Weigel act the scene with
the East Berlin Ensemble, though acting is a paltry word for
the marvel of her incarnation. As the body of her son was laid

before her, she merely shook her head in mute denial. The soldiers compelled her to look again. Again she gave no sign of recognition, only a dead stare. As the body was carried off, Weigel looked the other way and tore her mouth wide open. The shape of the gesture was that of the screaming horse in Picasso's *Guernica*. The sound that came out was raw and terrible beyond any description I could give of it. But, in fact, there was no sound. Nothing. The sound was total silence. It was silence which screamed and screamed through the whole theatre so that the audience lowered its head as before a gust of wind. And that scream inside the silence seemed to me to be the same as Cassandra's when she divines the reek of blood in the house of Atreus. It was the same wild cry with which the tragic imagination first marked our sense of life. The same wild and pure lament over man's inhumanity and waste of man. The curve of tragedy is, perhaps, unbroken.'[21]

4. WORSHIPPING AN ABSURD IMAGE

Perhaps the theatre with its rituals, and basis in group experience, comes nearest to a fourth fundamental of religion, namely worship. Christian belief has always seen men as 'wounded creatures', like Mother Courage, who can pray in their distress to a God above, who they believe shares in the sorrows of the earth. They may have experienced him in the worship of the church. The core of such worship, looked at externally, are rituals, and these may depend for their power on being symbolic.

One immediately apparent use of the rituals of the church, and a sign of their emotive power, was in unburdening man of his darkness, whether in the exorcising of devils, the release of the confessional, or in Holy Communion. It has been seen that some modern artists consciously think of their art as springing from personal need—'Art is for the artist sorrow, through which he frees himself for a further sorrow' (Kafka). And one thinks of the psychiatrist using art as a healing therapy. But whereas such healing may depend on free expression releasing suppressed experiences, for the artist this resolution depends on the achievement of order out of chaos by the use of significant forms. If the present situation is one of the breakdown of symbols—'the heap of broken images'—both the church and the artist face a problem.

In one sense this breakdown may be a good thing for both, in that it offers a tremendous clearing of the ground: the removal from church-art of the effete and medieval; a new chance for symbols to be more dynamic, by being more contemporary and more world-wide in their appeal. Yet the question arises—how can such renewal come about? Nobody, of course, knows, but some growth-points may be seen in surprising places: in the amorphous, the absurd and the inarticulate.

Modern man is afraid of the amorphous, whether it means feeling breaking the symmetry of logic, or the subconscious disturbing the order of the rational. Yet, as Wagner said, 'the function of the artist is to bring the unconscious part of human nature into consciousness within society'.[22] This however raises a problem: how can one give form to the amorphous and yet respect its nature? As N. F. Simpson commented:

> 'Sometimes I'm afraid that form distorts what is essentially amorphous. One's breaking faith with chaos.'[23]

Yeats was acutely aware of chaos—the centre that could not hold —and described the strange beast:

> 'A shape with lion body and the head of a man,
> A gaze blank and pitiless as the sun,
> Is moving its slow thighs, while all about it
> Reel shadows of the indignant desert birds.
> The darkness drops again.'[24]

Amorphous, because a symbol of a new age; feared, but not yet known and defined. Similarly amorphous, and equally expressive of the crisis of our age are the figures of Henry Moore—sprawling and unbalanced, suggestive of rock and hill. Moore has often defended this irregular quality:

> 'Sculpture . . . must have a feeling for organic form, a certain pathos and warmth. . . . Organic forms, though they may be symmetrical in their main disposition, in their reaction to environment, growth and gravity, lose their perfect symmetry.'[25]

Erich Neumann, as already noted, finds in Moore's figures an 'activation of the earth archetype', which 'compensates the crisis of our one-sided patriarchal culture' and 'symbolizes the essence of human relatedness' of man's 'social capacity, and the growing consciousness of the unity of mankind'. If Moore is, however, helping a 'new age into being',[26] none of his sculptures suggests an easy entrance. Significantly, he once claimed that:

'There is one quality I find in all the artists I admire most . . . a disturbing element, a distortion, giving evidence of a struggle of some sort. . . . One must try to find a synthesis, to come to terms with opposite qualities. . . . In great art this conflict is hidden, it is unsolved. . . . All that is bursting with energy is disturbing . . . not perfect. It is the quality of life.'[27]

If the amorphous means the pain of new life, the fitting commentator may be the waiting tramp:

'Astride of a grave and a difficult birth. Down in the hole, lingeringly, the grave-digger puts on the forceps. We have time to grow old. The air is full of our cries.'[28]

We have entered the realm of the absurd. The absurd has long roots: in Dostoievsky's *Idiot* and in Yeats' *Crazy Jane*, in Joyce's 'Nighttown' and in Kafka's nightmares, in the Surrealists' paintings and in the French existentialists' sense of 'the absurdity of it all'. The rising note of agreement among them is in denying the accepted explanations, both traditional and contemporary, of life's problems. There is no answer in the arts as man found in the past. The Orator in Ionesco's *The Chairs* enters looking like 'the typical painter and poet of the last century' and 'unreal'. When he turns to speak to the rows of empty chairs, one realizes that he can only make moans and guttural sounds, and scribble meaningless letters on the board.[29] Neither is there any answer in traditional religion. The tramps, Vladimir and Estragon, wait in vain on the rubbish dump:

VLADIMIR: What does he do, Mr. Godot? (*Silence*) Do you
          hear me?
BOY: Yes sir.
VLADIMIR: Well?
BOY: He does nothing, sir.
     (*Silence*.) . . .

VLADIMIR (*softly*): Has he a beard, Mr. Godot?
    BOY: Yes, sir.
VLADIMIR: Fair or . . . (*he hesitates*) . . . or black?
    BOY: I think it's white, sir.
        (*Silence*).
VLADIMIR: Christ have mercy on us!
        (*Silence*).[30]

Yet equally there is no authority in the accepted authority of the present: in science and sense experience. The inanimate, when it intrudes, is peculiarly alien and unpredictable. 'Things are divorced from their names,' says a character of Sartre. 'They are there, grotesque, stubborn, huge, and it seems ridiculous to call them seats, or to say anything at all about them. I am in the midst of things—nameless things.'[31] Art, religion and science, then, are equally absurd: man is in a universe where 'nothing, absolutely nothing, justifies his existence'.

The 'nothing' is misleading. Having asserted that the accepted frameworks of thought and interpretation are totally incapable of giving meaning for contemporary man, most of these artists do not rest there. Clearly, they make no attempt to provide any answer in new conceptual terms. Instead, they implicitly affirm the existence of other ways of knowing than the rational, by offering us the rawness of their individual experience, in deliberately irrational forms, so that both the experiences and the way of expressing it are shocking.

This shock has made good theatre. An illuminating study of it is Martin Esslin's *The Theatre of the Absurd*. Structurally, he points out, these plays are only unconventional in that they offer, not a narrative, but a symbol: the action 'gradually builds up the complex pattern of the poetic image that the play expresses. The spectator's suspense consists in waiting for the gradual completion of this pattern which will enable him to see the image as a whole.' These poetic images have a healing force for the spectator who, 'confronted with the madness of the human condition, is enabled to see his situation in all its grimness and despair. Stripped of illusions and vaguely felt fears and anxieties, he can face this situation consciously.' As for the dramatist himself, he stands outside any 'generally known and universally accepted metaphysical system', and all he can offer is 'an individual human being's in-

tuition of the ultimate realities as he experiences them'. So the
absurd points forward to the second half of this book:

> 'In trying to deal', continues Esslin, 'with the ultimates of the
> human condition not in terms of intellectual understanding
> but in terms of communicating a metaphysical truth through
> a living experience, the Theatre of the Absurd touches the
> religious sphere. There is a vast difference between *knowing*
> something to be the case in the conceptual sphere and *experien-*
> *cing* it as living reality. The Theatre of the Absurd, paradoxical
> though this may appear at first sight, can be seen as an attempt
> to communicate the metaphysical experience behind the scien-
> tific attitude, and, at the same time, to supplement it by round-
> ing off the partial view of the world it presents, and integrating
> it in a wider vision of the world and its mystery. . . .'[32]

In the face of mystery, man may be inarticulate. An outstanding discussion of the inarticulate, of the problems of non-
communication, is given by Schoenberg's opera *Moses and Aaron*.
Moses can be put alongside Orpheus, Dr. Faustus, and Mother
Courage to carry the burden of a theme. Strangely, all four are
the work of modern Germans; though they all lived a good deal
outside Germany, three were exiles, and Schoenberg insisted:

> 'I have at last learned the lesson that has been forced upon
> me . . . and I shall not ever forget it. It is that I am not a Ger-
> man, not a European, indeed perhaps scarcely a human being,
> at least the Europeans prefer the worst of their race to me, but
> I am a Jew.'[33]

And so his opera was based on an archetypal figure of his people's
history.

Schoenberg broadly follows the Bible story, but with a different
emphasis. The artist-priest, the Leader of the People, is Aaron.
He has a happy fluency in talking to the masses; he has a quick
facility with signs, symbols and rituals—the staff turned into a
snake, Moses' hand made leprous, the Nile water turned into a
blood, and he allows the worship of the Golden Calf. Moses
stands in the sharpest contrast and conflict with him. Moses is
essentially inarticulate—a fact symbolized in the opera, by his
not singing, but using only a heightened, cadenced voice. He
attacks Aaron's policies in every way he can. He is against his use

of signs: 'No image', he cries, 'can give you an image of the unimaginable.' Above all, he is horrified by the Golden Calf: 'Away
you image of the impossibility of enclosing the boundless in a
picture.' He refused to give God a mask. It was this perplexed
sense of the impossibility of explaining about, and also of
approaching to, so infinite a God as he had known in the Burning
Bush, that lies at the core of Moses' experience:

> 'Inconceivable because invisible;
> because immeasurable;
> because everlasting;
> because eternal;
> because omnipresent;
> because omnipotent.'

Moses is in despair when he finds Aaron leading the People by
the pillar of fire at night, and the pillar of smoke by day. Left
alone, he falls helpless to the ground.

> 'Thus am I defeated, thus all I thought was madness, and
> cannot and must not be spoken. O Word, Word, Word that I
> lack.'[34]

'O word, word, word that I lack.' These words mean a double
failure. A failure for the opera, for it breaks off here and Schoenberg found himself unable to finish it. A failure for Moses, yet it
is a failure of the richest importance, for it raises afresh all the
problems of art and communication, of symbols and experience
which the first part of this book has been about. It began by
suggesting the terror and disturbance of the new and of art; it
ends by touching on an experience of the numinous—of a man
standing in awe before an unknown god. 'The fright of the mind
before the unknown created not only the first gods, but also the
first art.'[35] We have looked at the art, now we must turn to the
gods.

REFERENCES

I. STEINER, G.: *The Death of Tragedy*, op. cit. This book offers an
outstanding discussion of the problem of myth and the modern
writer.

2. ELIOT, T. S.: From his review of Joyce's *Ulysses* in *The Dial*, November 1923. Quoted from DREW, E.: *T. S. Eliot: The Design of His Poetry* (Eyre and Spottiswoode, 1950).*

3. STEINER, G.: op. cit., pp. 322–3.

4. SPENDER, S.: *The Creative Element* (Hamish Hamilton, 1953), pp. 11–12.

5. LAWRENCE, D. H.: *Last Poems*. To be found in DE SOLA PINTO & ROBERTS (eds.): *The Complete Poems of D. H. Lawrence* (Heinemann, 1964). From his poem, 'Bavarian Gentians', p. 697.*

6. RILKE, R. M.: *Selected Works*. Volume II: *Poetry*. Tr. by J. B. Leishman (Hogarth, 1960).* From the *Sonnets to Orpheus*:
   Second Part: XII: 'Choose to be changed. . . .' p. 274.
   XIII: 'Anticipate all farewells. . . .' p. 275.
   First Part: XXVI: 'You that could sound till the end . . .' p. 265.
   The latter sonnet is also contained in RILKE (Penguin Modern European Poets), op. cit., p. 67.

7. SCHWITTERS, K.: See JUNG, C. G. (Aniela Jaffé), op. cit., p. 253.

8. OSBORNE, J.: *Look Back in Anger* (Faber, 1957), pp. 53, 55, 56.*

9. JOYCE, J.: *Ulysses*, op. cit., pp. 625, 627.

10. D'ARBAUD, J.: *The Beast of the Vaccarés*. Contained in SAURAT, D. (ed.): *Angels and Beasts—New Short Stories From France* (Westhouse, 1947).

11. KANDINSKY, W.: Quoted from JUNG, C. G. (Aniela Jaffé), op. cit., p. 254.

12. RILKE, R. M.: *Selected Poems* (Penguin Modern European Poets), op. cit. From the *Duino Elegies*: The Ninth Elegy, p. 64.*

13. RILKE, R. M.: Quoted from HELLER, E.: *The Disinherited Mind* (Bowes & Bowes, 1952). From the chapter 'Rilke and Nietzsche, with a Discourse on Thought, Belief, and Poetry'. See Penguin edition, p. 129.*

14. KLEE, P.: *On Modern Art*. Quoted from JUNG, C. G. (Aniela Jaffé), op. cit., p. 263.

15. MANN, T.: *Dr. Faustus*. Tr. H. T. Lowe-Porter (Secker, 1949), pp. 268–9.*

16. RILKE, R. M.: See HELLER, E.: op. cit., p. 140.

17. KAFKA, F.: *The Castle*. Tr. Willa & Edwin Muir (Secker, 4th ed. 1947), p. 77. Also in Penguin Modern Classics.*

18. STEINER, G.: op. cit., pp. 319, 353.

19. NIETZSCHE. F. W.: Quoted from HELLER, E.: op. cit., pp. 141, 140.

20. LAWRENCE, D. H.: *Last Poems*, op. cit., p. 701.

21. STEINER, G.: op. cit., pp. 353–4.

22. WAGNER, R.: From DONINGTON, R.: *Wagner's 'Ring' and its Symbols—the music and the myth* (Faber, 1963), p. 24.*

23. SIMPSON, N. F.: Author of *One Way Pendulum; A Resounding Tinkle* (Faber, 1960).*

24. YEATS, W. B.: *Selected Poetry*, op. cit. From the poem 'The Second Coming'.

25. MOORE, H.: *Henry Moore on Sculpture*, op cit. From 'The Nature of Sculpture', p. 58, and 'Unit One', p. 70.

26. NEUMANN, E.: *The Archetypal World of Henry Moore*, op. cit., p. 129.

27. MOORE, H.: op. cit. From 'The Hidden Struggle', pp. 91–6.

28. BECKETT, S.: *Waiting for Godot* (Faber, 1956), Act II (p. 90, in paperback ed.).*

29. IONESCO, E.: *The Chairs* in *Plays* (vol. I) (Calder and Boyars, 1958).*

30. BECKETT, S.: op. cit.

31. SARTRE, J. P.: *The Diary of Antoine Roquentin*. Tr. Lloyd Alexander (Lehmann, 1949), p. 169. Also available in Penguin as *Nausea*.*

32. ESSLIN, M.: *The Theatre of the Absurd* (Eyre and Spottiswoode, 1962).* From the final chapter: 'The Significance of the Absurd', pp. 290–314 (pp. 304, 302, 293, 310). It is of special interest for the second half of this book that Ionesco has had psychic experiences and is interested in Zen Buddhism with its rejection of conceptual thinking.

33. SCHOENBERG, A.: *Letters*. Edited by Erwin Stein and tr. by Eithne Wilkins & Ernest Kaiser (Faber, 1964). Letter 63, p. 88. (S. was writing to his personal friend, Kandinsky, declining an invitation to teach at the Bauhaus.)

34. SCHOENBERG, A.: *Moses and Aaron*. For useful introductory accounts, which appeared when opera was first produced at Covent Garden, and for source of quotations from libretto: 1. STEINER, G.: 'Schoenberg's "Moses and Aaron"' in *Encounter*, June 1965, Vol. XXIV, No. 6, pp. 40–6.
2. TIPPETT, M.: 'Schoenberg's "Moses and Aaron"' in *The Listener*, July 29, 1965. For a full study see WÖRNER, K. H.: *Schoenberg's 'Moses and Aaron'* (Faber, 1963).*

35. WORRINGER, W.: *Abstraction and Empathy*, op. cit. Herbert Read's phrase: for the Bullock translation see pp. 131–2.

Biographical Notes

A quick guide to some of the less familiar artists mentioned in the text.

ACHEBE, Chinua (b. 1930). Nigerian novelist, famous for *Things Fall Apart* (1962) and *No Longer at Ease* (1963). Has been Director of External Broadcasting for Nigeria.

AICHINGER, Ilse (b. 1921 in Vienna). Her novel *The Greater Hope* (1948) is the story of some Jewish children in Austria, during the period of Nazi occupation, when some of her own relatives died in Polish concentration camps.

D'ARBAUD, Joseph (1874–1950). Provençal poet and novelist, who often wrote in the vernacular with a French translation.

ARP, Hans (Jean) (b. 1888 in Alsace). Painter and sculptor. Interest in mysticism. Co-founder of Dada movement.

AWOONER-WILLIAMS, George (b. 1935). Ghanaian poet. First volume, *Rediscovery*, appeared 1964.

BERGENGRUEN, Werner (b. 1892–1964). German novelist. Catholic. *A Matter of Conscience (Der Grosstyrann und das Gericht)* appeared in 1935.

BROCH, Hermann (1886–1951). Austrian novelist. Trained as an engineer. Lived in U.S.A. since 1938. Outstanding novels: *The Sleepwalkers* and *The Death of Virgil*.

CHIRICO, Georgio di (b. 1888). Italian painter. Founded the *Pittura Metafisica* movement.

COCTEAU, Jean (1891–1963). French poet, dramatist, artist and filmmaker. Films include: *Beauty and the Beast, Orpheus*, and *The Eagle Has Two Heads*.

CORSO, Gregory (b. 1930). One of the 'beat' generation of young American poets. Friend of Allen Ginsberg. Spent three years in prison. *Gasoline* appeared 1958.

EISENSTEIN, Sergei (1898–1948). Born in Riga. Trained as engineer. Main films: *The Battleship Potemkin* (1925), *October* (1928), *Alexander Nevsky* (1938), *Ivan the Terrible*—only two parts of the intended trilogy were completed.

ELLISON, Ralph (b. 1914). American Negro writer. Studied music at Tuskegee Institute 1933–1936. His novel *The Invisible Man* appeared in 1952.

ERNST, Max (b. 1891). German painter. Interested in Dadaism and Surrealism. Experimented with 'collages' and 'frottages'.

GOTTHELF, Jeremias: pseudonym of the Swiss pastor Albrecht Bitzius (1797–1854), who did not start to write novels until he was 39. Became known in England through Ruskin's promotion of *Ulric the Farm Servant*.

GRAHAM, Martha (b. 1902). American dancer and choreographer. Her works—over 140 dances—include: *Primitive Mysteries, Dithyrambic, Errand into the Maze*, and *Appalachian Spring*.

HELLER, Joseph (b. 1923). American writer, who made his name with his first novel *Catch-22*: satirical study of conflict between bombardier and his commander.

HENZE, Hans-Werner (b. 1926). German composer. Co-operated with W. H. Auden in *Elegy for Dead Lovers*.

HESSE, Hermann (1877–1962). German novelist and poet, strongly interested in eastern thought. Novels include: *Steppenwolf, Death and the Lover, Magister Ludi* (Glasperlenspiel).

HINDEMITH, Paul (1895–1963). German composer. Emigrated to U.S.A. after Nazis had condemned his works. His last opera, *Harmony of the World*, (1957) is a study of the seventeenth-century scientist Kepler.

HU SHIH (1891–1962), Chinese writer. Studied in U.S.A. before returning to China to teach English at Peking University. Attempted to reform Chinese literature. Kept aloof from politics, but forced to flee when communists came to power. Died in Formosa.

IONESCO, Eugene (b. 1912). Rumanian, but writes in French. Dramatist of the 'Absurd' with such plays as *The Chairs, Rhinoceros, The Bald Prima-Donna* (in U.S. *The Bald Soprano*).

JIMINEZ, Juan (b. 1881–1965). Spanish poet, in exile after 1936. He received the Nobel Prize for Literature in 1956.

JONES, David (b. 1895). Welsh poet and painter. His difficult but outstanding works are: *In Parenthesis* and *The Anathemata*.

KANDINSKY, Wassily (1866–1944). Painter. Born in Moscow, but worked mainly in Germany. Closely associated with the *Blue Rider* group in Munich before 1914, and with the *Bauhaus* at Weimar from 1922.

KLEE, Paul (1879–1940). Swiss painter and etcher. Friend of Kandinsky. Work was condemned by Nazis as degenerate. Rich sense of fantasy.

KUROSAWA, Akira (b. 1910). Japanese film director, whose films include: *Rashomon* (1950), *Living* (1952), *The Seven Samurai* (1954), *The Lower Depths* (1958).

LOWELL, Robert (b. 1917). American poet, from aristocratic Boston family. Imprisoned as conscientious objector in Second World War. Renounced family's protestantism, and joined Catholic Church.

MARINI, Marino (b. 1901). Italian sculptor, working in bronze and wood. His key subject has been that of horse and rider.

MIRÓ, Joan (b. 1893). Spanish artist. Onetime interest in Surrealism. Abstract paintings, but with strong natural roots.

MONTHERLANT, Henri de (b. 1896). French novelist and dramatist. Skilled writer but with disturbing opinions: anti-democratic, anti-feminine, anti-bourgeois, and supported the occupying Germans 'pour le plaisir de trahir'.

MPHAHLELE, Ezekiel: Coloured South African, who left for Nigeria. Early years described in *Down Second Avenue* (1959). Chief work of criticism: *The African Image* (1962). An editor of *Black Orpheus*.

NASH, Paul (1889–1946). English painter. Official war artist in both World Wars. Memorable pictures of chalk landscape and dream fantasies.

NERUDA, Pablo (b. 1904). Chilean poet. Diplomatic service, and travelled widely. Became Communist. Profuse output, and imaginative understanding of South America.

NIETZSCHE, F. W. (1844–1900). German philosopher. Best known for *Thus Spake Zarathustra*, and his ideas of the Superman.

OWEN, Wilfred (1893–1918). Killed by machine-gun fire a week before the Armistice. Outstanding war poet.

PROKOFIEV, Sergei (1891–1953). Russian composer. Popularly known for *Peter and the Wolf*, and also for his opera *The Love of Three Oranges*, and his ballet music for *Romeo and Juliet*. Composed film music for Eisenstein.

RAY, Satyajit: Began as a commercial artist in Calcutta, before his career as a film director. Consistent series of successful films, since the *Apu Trilogy* in the 'fifties. Has won awards at Edinburgh, Venice and Cannes ('the most human document').

RILKE, Rainer Maria (1875–1926). Born in Prague of German descent. Brought up in the manner of a girl; then suffered five years at a military school. Important influences have been his study of art history, his visits to Russia, and his contacts with the sculptor Rodin. Unhappy marriage. Completed the *Duino Elegies*, and wrote all the 55 *Sonnets of Orpheus* within three weeks of February 1922. Said to have died of the prick of a rose thorn.

ROBBE-GRILLET, Alain (b. 1922). Advocate of the French 'new novel'. Stress on material objects rather than plot or character. Wrote the scenario for Alain Resnais' film, *Last Year at Marienbad*.

SCHOENBERG, Arnold (1874–1951). Jewish composer. Born in Vienna but emigrated to U.S.A. in 1934. Famous for his development of serial music, based on 12 tones. Friend of Kandinsky and Kokoschka. Music condemned by Hitler as 'degenerate'.

SCHWITTERS, Kurt (1887–1948). German artist, concentrating on 'collages'. Made three structures from rubbish, as described in text.

SENGHOR, Léopold Sédar (b. 1906). Poet. One of the outstanding exponents of *négritude*. In 1960, installed as first President of the Republic of Senegal.

SPENDER, Stephen (b. 1909). Poet and critic, who became known in the 'thirties. Interesting autobiography: *World Within World* (1951).

TIPPETT, Sir Michael (b. 1905). As well as *A Child of Our Time*, he has composed orchestral music, and two operas, *The Midsummer Marriage* (1952) and *King Priam* for the opening of the new Coventry Cathedral (1962).

UPDIKE, John (b. 1932). American novelist. Before *Run, Rabbit, Run*, he had written *The Centaur* and *The Poorhouse Fair*.

WEISS, Peter: Born in Germany but emigrated in 1934 to Sweden. His latest play, after *Marat*, is about the Auschwitz concentration camp and the Frankfurt trial. He has announced his conversion to Marxism-Leninism.

WHITE, Patrick (b. 1912). Studied in England, but essentially an Australian novelist. Main works: *The Tree of Man*, *Riders in the Chariot*, and his latest *The Solid Mandala*.

WILLIAMS, William Carlos (1883–1963). American writer. English father and Puerto Rican mother. Medical training. Key dictum: 'no ideas but in things'. Outstanding work: long poem *Paterson*.

BELIEF

James L. Henderson

Introduction

THE word 'Belief' can denote attitudes ranging from absolute faith to hesitant hypothesis, from certainty to surmise. Anywhere along this continuum lies the point at which a particular man or woman may feel driven to exclaim: 'This concerns me ultimately —this is the kind of creature I believe I am.' It is the nature of this continuum during the last fifty years of the world's history, which is the subject of the last part of this book. The link between it and the first part is neatly expressed in the following quotation from Hendrick Kraemer's *World Cultures and World Religions*:

'Art, being in our present epoch of religious and philosophical diversity and atrophy, the most universal, easily understandable language between men of culture all over the world, and so being practically the substitute religion of today, is a great winner of souls.'[1]

This is a theme to which we shall return in Chapter V: meanwhile it only remains to declare with clarity and conviction that 'The one and only real and profound theme of the world and all human history—the theme to which all others are subordinate— remains the conflict between belief and unbelief' (Goethe). Belief in what? In the 'Power of Spirit over Things', as that great Indian statesman and philosopher Radhakrishnan has expressed it.

All the earliest known manifestations of belief have certain elements in common: they are the constants. Recent research in many different fields of scholarship 'has combined to suggest a new image of the fundamental unity of the spiritual history of mankind'.[2]

As the human species developed in different ways in different places during its evolution, so the religious constants tended to be overlaid, sometimes to the point of their complete obliteration, by the variables created from differing human and natural environments and sets of experience. The ultimate unity of all religions however is well illustrated through the following story, retold by Campbell:

'A man entered a wood and saw a chameleon on a tree. He reported to his friend: "I have seen a red lizard." He was firmly convinced that it was nothing but red. Another person visiting the tree said: "I have seen a green lizard." He was firmly convinced that it was nothing but green. But the man who lived under the tree said: "What both of you have said is true. But the fact is that the creature is sometimes red, sometimes green, sometimes yellow, sometimes has no colour at all".'[3]

'Every student of comparative mythology', writes Campbell, 'knows that when the orthodox man talks and writes of God the nations go asunder; the desi, the local, historical, ethical aspect of the cultural symbol, is taken with absolute seriousness, and the chameleon is green, not red. Whereas when the mystic talks, no matter what their desi, their words in a profound sense meet— and the nations too. The names of Shiva, Allah, Buddha and Christ lose their historical force and come together as adequate pointers and a way (marga) that all must go, but would transcend their time-bound, earth-bound faculties and limitations.'[4]

As has already been suggested, modern art has to a very large extent been playing the role of the world's spiritual chameleon: nor, as will be apparent from a careful scrutiny of the volume in this series on scientific discovery and invention, is that chameleon unknown in the laboratory and workshop:

'Are the modern civilizations to remain spiritually locked from each other in their local notions of the sense of the general tradition; or can we not now break through to some more profoundly based point and counterpoint of human understanding?'[5]

Seeking the answer to that question involves taking a look first at the creeds of the main traditional religions still extant, then considering those beliefs, usually defined as non-religious but which have been exerting influences as potent as any of the religions proper, examining such beliefs as do not fall into either of the previous two categories but which may contain a greater human significance than them both, and finally assessing the prospects of belief today. While attempting this exercise it is important to remember that:

'The structure of the human being is such that man cannot live his life or understand himself without some ultimate concern that he takes as the that-beyond-which-there-is-nothing of his world. This is indeed his god and the articulation of his life in terms of it is his religion.'[6]

Martin Luther spoke even more tersely four centuries ago: 'Now I say whatever your heart clings to and confides in, that is your god.'

REFERENCES

1. KRAEMER, HENDRICK: *World Cultures and World Religions* Lutterworth Press, 1960, p. 159.*
2. CAMPBELL, JOSEPH: *The Masks of God—Primitive Mythology* (Secker and Warburg), pp. 4 et seq.*
3. op. cit., p. 463. For an excellent discussion of the use of the word 'Belief' see *Religious Studies*, Vol. I, No. 1, October 1961, 'Belief "in" and Belief "that" ', by H. H. Price.
4. op. cit., p. 463.
5. op. cit., p. 4.
6. HERBERG, W.: 'God and the Theologians', *Encounter*, November 1963.

CHAPTER ONE

Traditional Creeds: Then and Now

'The faith of every individual is in accordance with his nature.
Man is of the nature of his faith: what his faith is, that is he.'

(Bhagavad-Gita XVII, 3)

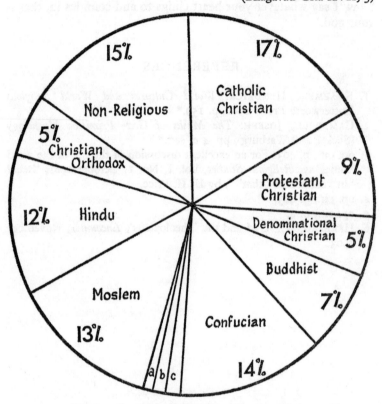

$a = $ *Jews* 0·4% $b = $ *Shintoist* 1·1% $c = $ *Taoist* 1·5%

How many believers in the creeds of the traditional religions are there in the world today? The subdivided circular diagram above[1] provides one answer: another may be given in millions.[2]

Christianity	904	(Made up of Roman Catholic 550, Protestant 217, Eastern Orthodox 137).
Islam	440	
Hinduism	350	
Buddhism	150	
Shintoism	51	
Taoism	50	
Judaism	12	
	1957	

But where in this second reckoning are the Confucians—14 per cent of the total according to the diagram, 420 million out of an estimated total world population of 3,000 million? Perhaps Confucianism is not strictly speaking a religion, but if, as we shall be doing later on, we accept Communism and Nazism, for example, as ultimate human concerns, there is good reason for including it. So let us add it in and settle for a round figure of 2,400 million believers. Any units of measurement are bound to be arbitrary, especially when we remember to distinguish between those who subscribe in ignorance or knowledge to all tenets of their religion and those who only believe in some of them. Institutional membership figures are inevitably misleading—for example, is it the 29 million baptized or the 9 million confirmed members of the Church of England who are to be counted as Christians? Or again, to what extent is the high percentage figure of 17 per cent for the Roman Catholic faith to be ascribed to the inclusion in it of many thousands of purely nominal converts in those lands strongly under Roman Catholic missionary influence? As T. S. Eliot remarked in *The Idea of a Christian Society*, 'To answer fully the question, what does A believe, one must know enough about A to have some notion of the level on which he is capable of believing anything.' In his book *Religious Behaviour*, Michael Argyle throws light on this conundrum: religious belief tends to vary with such different factors as age, sex, environment, class.

As regards world distribution of these various faiths, Christianity is mainly Western in its incidence, though including considerable areas in the New World, Africa and the Commonwealth which have come under European and missionary influence; Islam is to be found throughout the Middle East, North Africa, Pakistan and India; Hinduism almost entirely in India, Buddhism throughout South East Asia and Tibet, Shintoism in Japan, Taoism and Confucianism in China and Judaism in Israel and minutely but influentially in most of the white-populated parts of the world.

The beliefs of all these religions have been exposed during the last fifty years, ever more powerfully, to the influences of national-ism, socialism and secularism, and have undoubtedly been weak-ened and corroded by them, although at the same time this very process has led to the reform and restatement of traditional doc-trine. In proceeding to make some kind of estimate of the situa-tion in which their basic beliefs now stand, it is necessary to make a clear, though not absolute, distinction between the holding of them on the one hand by ordinary adherents and on the other by professionals such as priests, theologians or philosophers.

With reference to the first and far more numerous category, it should be remembered that for them the repetition of statements of belief, or even their tacit acceptance, very often means not intellectual assent but a kind of reassuring emotional habit, rarely scrutinized except at critical moments like birth, death or disaster, and even then only fleetingly. So what is any adherent of the following religions expected to believe in the second half of the twentieth century?

I. CHRISTIANITY

A Christian believes that his religion is uniquely true and that Jesus of Nazareth was not a but *the* Son of God, who 'for us men and our salvation, came down from Heaven and was incarnate by the Holy Ghost of the Virgin Mary and was made man and was crucified also for us under Pontius Pilate. He suffered and was buried and the third day He rose again according to the Scriptures and ascended into Heaven.' (The Apostles' Creed, forming part of the Anglican Communion Service.) He believes in the redemp-tion of man through the Crucifixion of Christ, who was and is essentially different from any other human being who has ever lived. It is therefore his duty to worship God and to pray to Him in His triple aspect as God the Father, God the Son and God the Holy Ghost. The Christian is fully committed to belief in what has been called this 'Scandal of Particularity'.

'God has revealed himself to man in Jesus Christ. What do we know from any other source of God?—Absolutely nothing.'[3] 'We gladly acknowledge the truths contained and emphasized in the great religions; but each of them is less than the Gospel of the unsearchable riches of Christ.'[4]

The Christian is also committed to belief in immortality in the sense of personal survival after death, the resurrection of the body and life everlasting; and to rewards for the living of a Christian life on earth, which may be denied to those who have sinned against God's Commandments as expressed in the Bible and through the teaching of the Churches. He is committed to belief, therefore, in some form of judgement, though not necessarily in hell-fire. Finally, the Christian is committed to belief in original sin, the notion that by definition there is a flaw in human nature, which can only be mended by God's forgiveness.

A permissible comment, therefore, might be that very few Christians today believe in the metaphysical truths which their religion proclaims, that a great number of them cling to some form of faith that God and Jesus will ensure that everything comes out all right in the end, that almost none of them accepts the dark view of human corruption and that most cultivate their moralities without appealing to Divine Christian sanction. Their secular, social and national loyalties all count for more than their religious ones.

'In effect, moral issues are now very rarely discussed in terms of the Christian concepts of Divine Law, sin, Christian charity and what is necessary to salvation. Indeed, the influence of religion on morality is now so inconspicuous that it is possible to know a person fairly well for many years and to be familiar with his views on a variety of moral problems, without being able to tell whether he is a Christian or not, or if so, to which sect of Christianity he subscribes.'[5]

Certainly, in respect of Western civilization, wherever located geographically, the following judgement must be accepted:

'It is clear that contemporary culture can no longer be regarded as Christian, since it is probably the most completely secular-ized form of culture that has ever existed.'[6]

'. . . We live in a thoroughly secularized age, that is to say, in an age in which most men and women simply take it for granted that this world—the world which we see and hear and smell and touch and taste during the brief span of time that stretches for each one of us from the cradle to the grave—is the only reality of which we need seriously take account.'[7]

Nevertheless, there are three positive aspects of the Christian believer's contemporary position: one is his concern for ecclesias-tical unity as experienced in the ecumenical movement of the non-Roman Catholic churches and chapels and even the drawing together of Roman Catholics and Protestants in the face of the common enemy of secularism. The second is the growth of his social conscience in regard to poverty and war, though this seems to have occurred at the expense of credal belief. Among many of those who still cherish a Christian outlook there are uneasiness and anxiety about the equivocal attitude of the Churches, both Roman Catholic and Protestant, towards the use of nuclear weapons, population control and the proper use of leisure in affluent societies. The third is the clarity with which there has been exposed the division between the extreme modernist Pro-testant Christian position and that of the traditional one. As Eric Mascall has pointed out, the former is a kind of secularized theology, the latter a theology of the secular. Extreme modernism, while affirming the Creed that Jesus Christ was born of the Virgin Mary, also maintains that this does not mean that He was in fact born of the Virgin Mary but that God has acted in history and that monogamous marriage is civilization's most important social in-stitution. As Mascall comments, 'I think that the reaction of many people to this recommendation must be to object: "Well, if that is what you mean, why not say so?" '[8] The position of the latter is again succinctly defined by Mascall himself in the follow-ing words: 'The world is real and precious because it is created and sustained by God, but it is not the ultimate reality or the supreme value because it is not God Himself; man on his bodily side is the highest product of biological evolution but because he is spirit as well as body he is a little lower than the angels; while he is born into this world, his ultimate destiny lies beyond this world in eternal life with God; a theology of the secular will say that this world is itself finally to be transformed into a state of unimaginable splendour and glory with all its goodness perfected and all its imperfection done away—these are the liberating and exhilarating claims which such a theology will use to interpret the hopes and fears, the achievements and failures of a secularized world that has forgotten its true nature and of secularized men who never knew theirs.'

2. JUDAISM

The Jew, whether Orthodox or Liberal, is committed to a belief in God's transcendental unity as uniquely revealed to His Chosen People, to a belief that this revelation is discernible in the patterns of Divine Providence at work in history. He believes that by means of worship, the strict keeping of the Jewish Sabbath and through other forms of ritual, he can learn the Will of God and acquire the strength to obey it. He is theoretically committed to a belief in immortality: but many Jews appear to regard this latter in a symbolic fashion. The knowledge of good and evil he finds in the Law—*Torah*, and much of the practice of his ethical monotheism is strict to the point of legalistic. At no time more than in the twentieth century, most tragically at the hands of Hitler, he and his brother Jews have suffered the fate of scapegoats of society. The emergence of the state of Israel has been at once the positive outcome of and the negative reaction to those same forces, already noticed as operating on Christian belief, namely nationalism, socialism and secularism. The present position of Judaism looks something like this: first, Orthodox Jewry with its precise accent on belief in the unity of the Godhead, no great sense of sin and a conviction that, if set about in the right way, the law can in fact be observed from youth onwards: secondly, liberal Jewry, among whom are to be found some who are almost Christian in outlook and some who are, philosophically speaking, mere theists. In spite of these quite significant differences, Jews the world over enjoy a striking sense of social cohesion, of belonging to a fraternity.

3. ISLAM

A Moslem believes that Mohammed, the Founder of Islam, though the greatest of religious prophets, was a mortal man, that there is one supreme God—Allah—to whose will all must submit, that he must be worshipped but without idols, ceremonies or priests. 'He believes in a Creator completely separated from his Creation and in the survival of the individual after death. His attitude to life is essentially positive and individualistic and it follows that both he and his Creator must have a separate and permanent existence.'[9]

'The Good Life is one of disciplined submission, abstemious in food and drink, though not in sexual matters, and motivated by a very definite paradise.'

It is worth noting here that the Shi'i form of Islam as the official religion of a Persian national state in the sixteenth century was followed in the nineteenth by a secession from it—the Bahai movement. This is a missionary religion, which addresses itself not only to Moslems but to all human beings of whatever faith. It combines the idea of the Imams themselves being successive incarnations of God with a liberal kind of theological Unitarianism.

Nevertheless, there is a stark contrast between contemporary acquiescence in or actual worship of nationalism, socialism and secularism and the traditional affirmation of Islamic faith: 'God is not to be inquired of as to what He does.' Credal pretension and political loyalty, especially in the Arab World, are uneasy bedfellows.

4. HINDUISM

A Hindu can be said to believe in almost anything, and in this religion more than in any other there is a vast difference between popular and esoteric versions of the faith. Sticking to the popular, it is probably still true to say that many, though a diminishing number, of Hindus still believe in the caste system of the Brahmins—the priestly class, Ksatriyas—warriors and noblemen, Vaisyas—merchants, business and craftsmen, Sudras—serfs doing manual jobs. Great inroads, however, have already been made into these articles of faith by industrialization and urbanization. Secondly, the Hindu believes in the doctrine of re-incarnation, the idea that the individual soul has many successive lives, the nature of which is determined by conduct in the previous one, i.e. the notion of Karma.

Hindu beliefs about Divinity are again divided between fairly crude but persistent polytheistic concepts and an extremely subtle metaphysics of consciousness in which Atman and Brahman are seen as the immanent and transcendent aspects of Deity. Both, however, are pantheistic in the sense that everything is God and that God is everything. 'Thou art That.' The bond which unites man to this absolute reality he believes to be established and cultivated by means of Yoga—a complex series of techniques such as breath control and dieting through which man can obtain union with absolute reality and into which as the climax of his search his individual being finally and utterly merges. Indeed, this is perhaps a good point at which to emphasize that in Hinduism the individual has no ultimate role, as he has within the belief frameworks of Christianity, Judaism and Islam. Also, in passing over from these three religions to Hinduism, Buddhism, Taoism and Confucianism, our enquiry must of necessity change key completely. Whatever the differences between the first three, they are all monotheistic religions with a strong concern for the life of the here and now, a conviction that the events of this life matter supremely. The contrast between them and the Hindu outlook is well demonstrated by the following lines from the *Bhagavad Gita*:

'Never the spirit was born; the spirit shall cease to be never;
Never was time when it was not; End and Beginning are dreams.
Birthless and deathless and changeless remaineth the spirit for ever,
Death hath not touched it at all, dead though the house of it seems.'

Such words illustrate further how dramatic is the clash in modern India between the fatalistic view of the Hindu scriptures and the clamouring need for social reform in secular terms.

5. BUDDHISM

A Buddhist, like a Hindu, believes in reincarnation and Karma but he does not believe in caste, and Buddhism itself in various forms, unlike Hinduism, has spread throughout the Far East. A Buddhist believes 'that man suffers because of his craving to possess and keep for ever things which are essentially impermanent. Chief among these is his own person, for this is his means of isolating himself from the rest of life, his castle into which he can retreat and from which he can assert himself against external affairs. He believes that this fortified and isolated position is the best means of obtaining happiness; it enables him to fight against change, to strive to keep pleasant things for himself, to shut out suffering and to shape circumstances as he wills. In short, it is his means of resisting life. The Buddha taught that all these, including his castle, are essentially impermanent and that as soon as man tries to possess them they slip away; this frustration and the desire to possess is the immediate cause of suffering; but he went further than this, for he showed that the fundamental cause is the delusion that man can isolate himself from life.

'A false isolation is achieved by identifying himself with his castle, the person, but because this castle is impermanent, it has no abiding reality, it is empty of any "self-nature" (*atta*) and is no more the Self than any other changing object. What, then, is the Self? The Buddha remained silent when asked this question, but he taught that man will find out only when he no longer identifies himself with his person, when he no longer resists the external world from within this fortification, in fact, when he makes an end to his hostility and his plundering expeditions against life. Buddha proclaimed the unity of all living things and charged his followers to replace this hostility by Divine compassion (*Karma*). The practice of this teaching brings the disciple to the state of *Nirvana*, the end of everything and the extinction of selfishness, the condition of eternal bliss which no words can describe.'[10]

Buddhism itself is still best summarized by rehearsing the four Noble Truths.

(1) To live is to suffer: suffering and frustration come to all: no one escapes pain, separation, sorrow, death.

(2) The cause of suffering is desire; that is, attachment to

people, things and to life itself, especially to life conceived as a separate individual existence.

(3) Suffering ceases when desire ceases: we must therefore break all the chains of attachment.

(4) The way to destroy desire is to follow the eightfold path of right views, right desires, right speech, right action, right livelihood, right effort, right awareness, right meditation.

Like the other traditional religions, Buddhism has been increasingly exposed to the forces of nationalism, socialism and secularism, but for reasons which may have to do with the essence of its doctrine, it seems less affected by them than others and even seems to have something to offer by way of a kind of challenge to them—not least in the Western world. This theme will be resumed later in the next chapter.

6. CONFUCIANISM AND TAOISM

In next considering the common man's beliefs in China, it is well to begin by recognizing that behind the specific Confucian and Taoist outlooks which have probably always been confined, so far as their philosophical content is concerned, to the educated minority, their general flavour must have penetrated, however faintly, downward to the masses. These, however, have been more thoroughly affected by early primitive nature religions and then after the sixth or seventh centuries by Buddhism, in the nineteenth century and after by Christian missionary teaching, and over the last few decades by Communism. Traditionalism and utilitarianism, it might be suggested, are two words which could be easily thought of as linking the esoteric and exoteric sides of religion in China.

Central to the teaching of Confucius, and by no means necessarily ruling out belief in some kind of Deity, is the doctrine of man. This takes the form of a belief, optimistic in the extreme, that in every human being there reside benevolence, justice, propriety and wisdom and that these qualities can be cultivated by obedience to the law which their practice involves. Central to Taoism is the notion that there is in life 'a Way things are' and 'a Way they work'—Tao, and that by adjusting himself to it man fulfils himself and communicates and identifies with the known personal element in deity. The classical pair of opposites, *Yang* and *Yin*, together with light and dark, full and empty, these and countless other pairs of opposites are the two sides of the Way on which man can experience the golden mean. Three quotations do more than pages of descriptive writing to convey the essence of these two outlooks:

(1) 'It is not truth that makes man great but man that makes truth great.'
(2) 'If the wrong man uses the right means, the right means work in the wrong way.'
(3) 'Muddy water, left to stand, becomes clear.'

As Bouquet has said, 'Whether rightly or wrongly, a people steeped in Confucian thought will always naturally tend towards an optimistic anthropology. The sense of human inadequacy goes only with an intense perception of the transcendent holy God. Chinese wisdom, with its vague theism and its preoccupation with human relationships, is in consequence less sin-conscious than Hebrew and Christian prophetism, and also less world-negating than the thought of India.'[11]

7. SHINTOISM

A Shintoist is one who believes in the non-Buddhist religions of Japan, the Chinese word *Shin-to* simply meaning the way of the gods—*to* itself being the same as *Tao*, the way. Between 1870 and 1945, however, Shintoism became closely identified with Japanese nationalism. This led to a separation between state Shintoism and sect Shintoism:

'The fundamental idea in Shinto is that of *Kami*, which may perhaps be rendered as "the sacred", but which is also the equivalent of the Polynesian *mana* and of the Latin *numen*.'[12]

After the defeat of Japan in the Second World War and the secularization of the Mikado, it is sect Shinto which has survived to some purpose.

REFERENCES

1. *Duden-Lexikon,* Band 3, p. 1778.
2. KELLETT, A.: *The World's Living Religions* (Epworth Press, 1963).*
3. BARTH, KARL: *The Knowledge of God and the Service of God* (Hodder and Stoughton, 1938), p. 43.*
4. Statement of the Lambeth Conference, 1930.
5. WHITELEY, C. H. and W. N.: *The Permissive Morality* (Methuen, 1964).
6. DAWSON, CHRISTOPHER: *Mediaeval Essays* (Sheed and Ward, 1953), p. 9.
7. MASCALL, ERIC: 'Faith and Fashion', *The Listener,* 23 December 1965.
8. op. cit.
9. GRIFFITHS, SIR PERCIVAL: *Modern India* (Benn, 1965).*
10. WATTS, ALAN W.: *The Spirit of Zen* (John Murray, 1936).*
11. BOUQUET, A. C.: *Comparative Religion* (Penguin, 1955, 4TH EDN), p. 190.
12. op. cit., p. 194.

CHAPTER TWO

Modern Interpreters

'Metaphysical thought: reflection trained on mystery.'
(GABRIEL MARCEL: *Being and Thinking*)

WHILE nationalism, socialism and secularism have been eroding all of these traditional religions in their popular forms, as briefly sketched above, this tendency has to some extent been offset by the lives and thoughts of a number of men and women who, still loyal to their respective faiths, have during the last fifty years sought to reinterpret them in the light of modern knowledge and experience. Some words of appraisal and assessment of a few of them may serve as a stimulus to further exploration of their own ideas and those of their peers.

GABRIEL MARCEL (b. 1890) is a Roman Catholic philosopher whose distinctive note is sounded in three tones: first there is his admirable common-sense approach to deep problems by means of the skilful use of everyday, human experience; secondly there is his subtle metaphysics; thirdly there is his by no means unsuccessful attempt to reach the non-philosophic mind by means of his dramatic works.

Marcel's philosophy of experience strikes the ear as a direct answer in existential terms (see Chapter III) to Sören Kierkegaard's prophetic comment:

'Experience, it is said, makes man wise. That is very silly talk. If there was nothing beyond experience it would simply drive him mad.'[1]

Experience, argues Marcel, is not a spring-board—'It seemed to me that it must suck down the spirit like a quicksand'; in contrast to it there is 'great music and drama—glimpses of a

higher unity—something beyond experience—a kind of knowledge which transcends mere objectivity'.

'The real question seemed to me to find out of what kind was
that existence which Idealism vainly attempted to deny and
whether, in the last analysis, its existence did not vastly exceed
its outward appearances.'[2]

Like other thinkers of the twentieth century, Marcel recognizes
the connection between 'abstraction' in life and thought and the
phenomena of 'mass-violence'—when, for example, a human
being is treated not as a worker but as mere 'labour'. (See Chapter
III, p. 176.)

Marcel has shown an eloquent awareness of many sides of
modern man's dilemma, his 'fanaticized consciousness', 'the moral
blood-poisoning of his non-significant toil', his inclination to remark 'I am no good, but neither is my neighbour.'[3]

'I need hardly insist on the stifling impression of sadness produced by this functionalized world. It is sufficient to recall the
dreary image of the retired official, or those suburban Sundays
when the passers-by look like people who have retired from
life.'[4]

Above all, Marcel makes a vital distinction between a problem
and a mystery: for him life is not a problem to be solved but a
mystery to be experienced. A mystery is defined as a problem
which encroaches on 'itself', and it is in the elaboration of this
thought with regard to the philosophy of existence that Marcel
comes nearest to building a bridge between Christian and non-
Christian believers: his philosophy is

'perfectly well able to affect souls who are strangers to all
positive religion of whatever kind: this recognition, which takes
place through certain modes of human experience, in no way
involves adherence to any given religion; but it enables those
who have attained it to perceive the possibility of revelation in
a way which is not open to those who have never ventured
beyond the frontiers of the realm of the problematical and who
have therefore never reached the point from which the mystery
of being can be seen and recognized.'[5]

That is the point of hope, and, Marcel points out, 'the only genuine hope is hope in what does not depend on ourselves. Hope appears as though piercing through time . . . it does not say what is going to happen, but it affirms as if it saw . . . hope is linked with a certain candour, a certain virginity untouched by experience. It belongs to those who have not been hardened by life.'[5]

In July 1950, Marcel delivered a lecture called *The Drama of the Soul in Exile*, which might well constitute a sub-title for the whole section of this book on Belief.[6] Marcel explains how it is within the dramatist's power to create a 'cosmos from chaos', to bring hope into what would otherwise be a mere series of 'one damn thing after another'. He studies the soul 'which has become a stranger to itself, which can no longer understand itself, which has lost its way' in the characters in *A Man of God*, *The Funeral Pyre* and *Ariadne*. Marcel essentially follows Shakespeare's method of holding a mirror up to nature in order to 'lead the spectator to the focal point in himself where his thought can proliferate, not on the abstract level but on the level of action, and enfold *all* the characters of a play without any decrease in their reality or in their irreducible individuality . . . to awaken or reawaken in us the consciousness of the infinite which is concealed in the particular.' Those last words epitomize Marcel's contribution to contemporary contemplative thought.

DIETRICH BONHOEFFER (1906–1944) was a German Protestant pastor, who was imprisoned and killed by the Nazis in 1944 because of his opposition to their regime. His Christian belief led him into many restatements, often in poetical form, of the Christian faith and also into action of a sufficiently political nature to procure for himself political persecution and assassination. He was a man of God pledged to resist all kinds of totalitarianism. His fate is of supreme importance to our understanding of belief in the twentieth century as it has been variously constellated between politics and religion. The story goes that in 1946 some Protestant German clergy wrote to Bonhoeffer's father asking him to join them in a protest against the local Social Democratic Party's decision to include his son's name among other anti-Hitler conspirators' names which were being used to re-name streets. Why? Because they did not wish the names of those of their brethren who had died as martyrs for their faith to be numbered among mere political conspirators. The old man replied tersely that his son had in fact quite plainly died as one of the conspirators and that he therefore saw no reason why he should falsify a fact. A memorial to him in the church at Flossenburg, the scene of his incarceration and hanging, carries this inscription:

'Dietrich Bonhoeffer, a witness among his brethren to Jesus Christ.'

Those brethren counted among their number officers, socialists and atheists—evidence clear as a bell that belief in the 'power of the spirit over things' (see p. 135) could be extended in practice as well as in theory for a believing Christian to non-believers, who shared in part at least his own poignant sense of the human predicament. Bonhoeffer's comments on this fact make arresting reading:

'I do not want to become a Saint but to learn how to believe . . . I am not naturally a religious spirit';

and from prison, he writes:

'I often ask myself why it is that a Christian instinct often attracts me more to those without religion than to the religious.'[7]

The focus of his politico-religious involvement in contemporary history is shown by the journey he undertook to Stockholm in May 1942, to contact the then Bishop of Chichester with a view to acquainting the British Government with the plans of the German Resistance Movement to kill Hitler. The desperate condition at that time of all those concerned with the fight against tyranny is underlined by the failure of his mission.

MARTIN BUBER (1878–1963) was a Jew, who by his writings and personal example did a very great deal to establish acceptable channels of communication between Judaism and other religious and philosophical outlooks. He achieved this through three media: his popularization of some of the most beautiful Hassidim stories and parables, the short but startlingly clear challenge of his book *I and Thou*, and lastly through his reflections on education in *Between Man and Man*. His has been one of the most profound explorations of what exactly it is that constitutes the tissue of human relationships: there is, according to Buber, an absolute distinction between an I-Thou and an I-it relationship, it being the quality of the former's nature which distinguishes man from the rest of creation because in a true I-Thou relationship there is always present that redemptive third in front of which both I and Thou bow down and which can alone give sanction and blessing to our union.

'On the far side of the subjective, on this side of the objective, on the narrow ridge where I and Thou meet, there is the Realm of "Between".

'But this is the exalted melancholy of our fate, that every Thou in our world must become an It.'

The only escape from this predicament is into the realm of the Between which belongs to those who have transcended their Body-Egos (see Chapter V). In his series of Educational Essays Buber has caught in two short paragraphs the whole secret of authority in education and because this illustrates so well why it is that he has won disciples all over the world they are quoted here in full:

'For the first time a young teacher enters the class room independently. . . . The class before him is like a mirror of mankind, so multiform, so full of contradictions, so inaccessible, he feels: "These boys—I have not sought them out; I have been put here and have to accept them as they are—but not as they now are in this moment, no, as they really are, as they can become. But how can I find out what is in them and what can I do to make it take shape?" And the boys do not make it easy for him. They are noisy, they cause trouble, they stare at him with impudent curiosity. He is at once tempted to check this or that trouble maker, to issue orders, to make compulsory the rules of decent behaviour, to say No, to say No to everything rising against him from beneath. And if one starts from beneath one perhaps never arrives above, but everything comes down. But then his eye meets a face, which strikes him. It is not a beautiful face, nor particularly intelligent; but it is a real face, or rather, the chaos preceeding the cosmos of a real face. On it he reads a question which is something different from the general curiosity: "Who are you? Do you know something? What do you bring? . . ."

'And he addresses this face. He says nothing very ponderous or important, he puts an ordinary, introductory question: "What did you talk about last in Geography? The Dead Sea? Well, what about the Dead Sea?" But there was obviously something not quite usual in the question, for the answer he gets is not the ordinary schoolboy answer: the boy begins to tell a story. . . . "And everything looked to me as if it had been created a day before the rest of creation"—unmistakably he had only in this moment made up his mind to talk about it. In the meantime his face has changed. It is no longer quite as chaotic as before. And the class has fallen silent. They all listen. The class too is no longer a chaos. Something has happened. The young teacher has started from above.'

SIR MUHAMMED IQUBAL (1874–1936) was an eminent Arabic poet but also, which is more to our immediate purpose, the man who set in motion the whole movement of the Moslem world towards a re-thinking and re-interpretation of the traditional teaching of Mohammed. Until well into the twentieth century only Western university-trained Moslems were aware of the meaning of modern historical criticism, philosophy and science. Iqubal's *Six Lectures on the Reconstruction of Religious Thought in Islam*, followed in 1948 by Shaykh Muhammed Ashraf's Journal, *The Islamic Literature*, did something to give religious and moral approval to the vast changes which were sweeping the Moselm world as it became increasingly exposed to the forces of nationalism, socialism and secularism.

'The tendency now is to repudiate the teaching of the past on fatalism, the inferiority of women, blind obedience to authority, lack of a healthy spirit of scepticism and a low public morality.'[8]

SARVEPALLI RADHAKRISHNAN (b. 1888) is a Hindu philosopher and Indian statesman who, together with scholars like the European Guénon and the Indian Coomeraswamy, has constructed many bridges in our time between Oriental and Occidental thought. The keynote of his message is expressed in the following remark:

'The world which had found itself as a single body is feeling for its soul.'

Two major works, *East and West in Religion* (1933) and *Eastern Religions and Western Thought* (1939), justify the following judgement of *The Times Literary Supplement* for May 3rd, 1934:

'The metaphysics of Radhakrishnan's Absolute Idealism represents a real fusion of East and West in so far as it boldly confronts the problem which haunted F. H. Bradley—that of the relation between the Absolute and the God of religious experience.'

His teaching is based on the classical Hindu tradition of synthesis and the organic unity of all things: its twofold goal is that of happiness on earth and salvation.

'Detachment of spirit and not renunciation of the world is what is demanded from us.'

Here Radhakrishnan is meeting the stock Western criticism of the Eastern outlook that it leads to apathy and quietism. In dealing with the philosophical problem of the Godhead Immanent and/or transcendent he goes a very long way to abolishing this dualism or rather to justifying its bipolarity and, in so doing, as will be seen later, comes close to much of what western psychology has had to report about the structure of human personality. (See Chapter V.)

'God, though immanent, is not identical with the world until the end. Throughout the process there is an unresolved residuum in God, but it finishes when we reach the end.' This problem which it is so hard to make verbal sense of, consists in the fact that what we use the word God for is both in us and outside us—a truth which none of us can comprehend except in so far as we ourselves become it. 'We are not through this process of self-realization abolishing our individuality but transforming it into a conscious term of the universal Being, an utterance of the transcendent Divine.'

Against the overweening pride of the western Ego Radhakrishnan issues this warning:

'There is in the self of man, at the very centre of his being, something deeper than the intellect, which is akin to the Supreme.'

What that 'something deeper' is we shall re-examine in Chapter V.

DAISETZ TEITARO SUZUKI (b. 1870), Professor of Buddhist Philosophy in the Otani University, Kyoto, Japan, has been the chief bridge between Buddhism, especially Zen Buddhism, and the West in the twentieth century. In his foreword to Suzuki's book, *An Introduction to Zen Buddhism*, Christmas Humphreys comments:

'Dr. Suzuki writes with authority. Not only has he studied original works in Sanskrit, Pali, Chinese and Japanese, but he has an up-to-date knowledge of Western thought in Germany and France as well as in the English which he speaks and writes so fluently. He is something more than a scholar. Though not a priest of any Buddhist sect he is honoured in their temples in Japan for his knowledge of spiritual things, which, as all who have sat at his feet bear witness, is direct and profound. When he speaks of the higher stages of consciousness he speaks as a man who dwells therein, and the impression he makes on those who enter the fringes of his mind is that of a man who seeks for the intellectual symbols wherewith to describe a state of awareness which lies indeed "beyond the intellect".'[9]

As a belief in this 'state of awareness which lies indeed beyond the intellect' is becoming a mark of the most up-to-date thought synthesis of East and West it is important at least to make its acquaintance here and now in the form of Zen Buddhism and subsequently in the esoteric teachings of Taoism. From the European side, and this can surely be no mere chance, Carl Gustav Jung has in both cases acted as the Western end of this bridge connecting Occident and Orient. For a profound exploration of the philosophical significance of this bridge there is no finer study than *The Destiny of The Mind: East and West* by W. S. Haas (Faber and Faber, 1956). In it the author expounds how it is 'that there can be no knowing without a correspondingly adequate state of being', and how 'consciousness must be placed above reason as the ultimate and superior datum'.

It is in his book *Mysticism, Christian and Buddhist* that Suzuki comes closest to forging a link between East and West. Comparing the Christian mysticism of the medieval Eckhardt with Buddhism he brings out clearly the contrasting *leitmotifs* of each: Crucifixion in the case of Christianity, enlightenment in the case of Buddhism.

'Whatever knowledge the philosopher may have, it must come out of his experience, and this experience is seeing.'[10]

Yes, but seeing what? Seeing things in their state of such-ness or is-ness, 'having a mind free from the bondage of its conditioning aggregates' (i.e. not being distracted by the context in which our bodies are). Yet being free from the tyranny of the mind's divine conditions does not mean that the conditions no longer exist. Here we are surely very close to that Existentialist predicament which our modern Western philosophers so anxiously explore; and Ulrich in Musil's *The Man without Qualities* resembles some-what those Zen Buddhist monks in search of *Satori* (enlighten-ment) of whom there are such countless puzzling anecdotes. We cannot do better than recount a couple here by way of gauging the degree to which we of the West are just beginning to open our ears to that non- but not anti-logical teaching of the East.

'A monk asked Joshu, "What would you say when I come to you with nothing?" Joshu said, "Fling it down on the ground." Protested the monk, "I said that I had nothing; what shall I let go?" "If so, carry it away," was the retort of Joshu.'

It is above all in the dilemma of the *Koan*, a kind of problem which cannot be made sense of logically, which nevertheless makes sense, that we perhaps come closest to seeing a way out of the 'metallic realm of the absurd' (Malraux), which threatens to suffocate us. For example 'a sound is made by the clapping of two hands. What sound is made by the clapping of one hand?' . . . 'Thus each Koan reflects the giant Koan of life, for to Zen the problem of life is to pass beyond the two alternatives of assertion and denial both of which obscure the truth.'[11]

'A long time ago a man kept a goose in a bottle. It grew larger and larger until it could not get out of the bottle any more; he did not want to break the bottle, nor did he wish to hurt the goose; how would you get it out?'

As Watts remarks:

'To Westerners these Koans may appear as pure rubbish, reminiscent of "why is a mouse when it spins?" But it will be noticed that all of these Koans involve one in some kind of dilemma; there is generally a choice between two alternatives, both of which are equally impossible. . . . One begins by trying to grapple with it intellectually; it is found to contain a certain kind of symbolism and analogy. Thus in the tale about the goose we find that the goose represents man and the bottle his circumstances; he must either abandon the world so as to be free of it, or else be crushed by it, but both of these alternatives are forms of suicide. What purpose is to be served by abandoning the world, and what can we achieve if we allow it to crush us? Here is the fundamental dilemma with which the Zen disciple is concerned and somehow he must find a way through. The moment he finds it there comes a flash of Satori: the goose is out of the bottle and the bottle is unbroken, for suddenly the disciple has escaped from the bondage of his own imaginary prison—the rigid view of life which he himself has created out of his desire for possession. Thus to the question "How shall I escape from the Wheel of Birth and Death?" a master replied: "Who puts you under restraint?" '[12]

It is significant that a London theatre recently put on a Zen play called *Kindly Monkeys* by Milton Hood Ward which attracted considerable attention. In it we find the following remark, ' "Let us help you out of the water or you will drown," said the kindly monkeys and put the fishes safely up the tree.'

RICHARD WILHELM (1873–1930) is probably less well known than the other thinkers mentioned in this chapter. His influence, however, on changing patterns of belief in the twentieth century, particularly as between East and West, is certainly as great as and may be greater than theirs. He was a German missionary, theologian and Sinologue, who lived and worked in Tsing Tai, China, from 1899 to 1921. Between 1922 and 1924 he was Counsellor at the German Legation in Peking and subsequently Professor of Chinese at Frankfurt am Main. His great service was the translation of and commentary on the *I Ching* or *The Book of Changes* and *The Secret of the Golden Flower—A Chinese Book of Life*. From them a flood of light is thrown on what we in the West would call the problem of chance and the nature of consciousness.[13]

In his Memorial Address 'In Memory of Richard Wilhelm' delivered in Munich, May 10th, 1936, Jung said:

'Anyone like myself, who has had the rare good fortune to experience in a spiritual exchange with Wilhelm the divinatory power of the *I Ching*, cannot for long remain ignorant of the fact that we have touched here an Archimedean point from which our Western attitude of mind can be shaken to its foundations.

'The science of the *I Ching* is not based on the causality principle' (see Chapter V) 'but on a principle hitherto unnamed because not met with among us which I have tentatively called the synchronistic principle. My occupation with the psychology of unconscious processes long ago necessitated my looking about for another principle of explanation because the causality principle seemed to me inadequate to explain certain remarkable phenomena of the psychology of the unconscious. Thus I found that there are psychic parallelisms which cannot be related to each other causally, but which must be connected through another sequence of events. This connection seemed to me to be essentially provided in the fact of their relative simultaneity, therefore the expression "synchronistic".'[14]

As this last quotation from Jung indicates, we have here a theme which will constantly be heard in succeeding chapters.

"In the midst of the clanging disharmony of the concert of European opinion, to hear the simple language of Wilhelm, the messenger from China, is a real blessing. One can see from it that it has been schooled in the plant-like naïveté of the Chinese mind, which is able to express profound things in simple language; it discloses something of the simplicity of great truth, the ingenuousness of deep meaning, and it carries to us the delicate perfume of the Golden Flower. Penetrating gently, it has set in the soil of Europe a tender seedling, for us a new presentiment of life and meaning, after all the spasm of arbitrariness and presumption.

'Towards the foreign culture of the East, Wilhelm displayed an extraordinarily large amount of modesty, something unusual in a European. He erected no barrier against it, no prejudices, no assumptions of knowing better, but instead, opened heart and mind to it. He let himself be gripped and shaped by it, so that when he came back to Europe, he brought us not only in his spirit, but also in his nature, a true image of the East. This deep transformation was certainly not won by him without great sacrifice, because our historical premises are so entirely different from those of the East. The keenness of

Western consciousness and its glaring problems had to soften before the more universal, more equable nature of the East, and Western rationalism with its one-sided differentiation had to yield to Eastern breadth and simplicity. To Wilhelm, these changes certainly meant not only a shifting of intellectual standpoint, but also an essential rearrangement of the component parts of his personality. The picture of the East he has given us, free as it was from ulterior motive and any trace of violence, could never have been created in such completeness by Wilhelm, had he not been able to let the European in himself slip into the background. If he had allowed East and West to clash against each other within him with an unyielding harshness, he could not have fulfilled his mission of providing us with a true picture of China.

'Wilhelm fulfilled his mission in every sense of the word. Not only did he make accessible to us the dead treasures of the Chinese mind, but, as I have pointed out, he brought with him its spiritual root, the root that has lived all these thousands of years, and planted it in the soil of Europe. With the completion of his task, his mission reached its climax, and, unfortunately, its end also. According to the law of *enantiodromia*,* so clearly understood by the Chinese, there grew out of the close of the one phase the beginning of its opposite. Thus, in its culmination, yang goes over into yin, and the positive is resolved into negative. I came near to Wilhelm only in the last years of his life, and then I could observe how, with the completion of his life-work, Europe and the European man drew closer and closer to him, *beset him in fact*. At the same time, there developed in him the feeling that he might be standing on the brink of a great change, a transformation whose nature, it is true, he could not clearly grasp. He only knew that he was faced with a decisive crisis. His physical illness went parallel with this spiritual development. His dreams were filled with Chinese memories, but they were always sad and dismal pictures that hovered before him, a clear proof that the Chinese contents had become negative.

'There is nothing that can be sacrificed for ever. Everything returns later in a changed form, and where so great a sacrifice has once taken place, when the sacrificed thing returns, there

* A conversion of something into its opposite.

must be ready a healthy and resistant body in order to be able to meet the shock of a great transformation. Therefore, a spiritual crisis of such dimensions often means death if it takes place in a body weakened by disease. For now the sacrificial knife is in the hand of him who has been sacrificed, and a death is demanded of him who was once the sacrificer.

'As you see, I have not withheld my personal ideas, because if I had not told how I experienced Wilhelm, how else would it have been possible for me to speak of him? Wilhelm's life-work is of so great a value to me because it explains and confirms so much of what I had been seeking, striving for, thinking and doing, in order to meet the psychic ills of Europe. It was a tremendous experience for me to hear through him in clear language, the things that had been dimly shadowed forth to me from out of the confusion of the European unconscious. As a matter of fact, I feel myself so very much enriched by him that it seems to me as if I had received more from him than from any other man, and this is the reason I do not feel it a presumption if I am the one to offer, on the altar of his memory, the gratitude and respect of all of us.'[15]

In concluding this chapter two reflections may be legitimate. The first is that a review of the traditional beliefs in their popular forms leads to the conclusion that they are all to be sharply distinguished from the secular faiths with the possible exception of Confucianism, and that they differ very greatly among themselves.

'Where one religion holds to a belief that there have been many incarnations of God, it is difficult to conceive of a religion which completely denies this as being the fulfilment of the *first*. Where one religion is committed to the pre-supposition that man is tied to a series of purposeless existences by a causal chain which is burdensome, and the other religion firmly maintains that man has but one earthly life and that it is an opportunity for joyous development as a child of God, it would appear to be extremely unlikely that the latter is a logical fulfilment of the former.'[16]

Our second reflection is that in the theory and practice of a number of modern thinkers, each loyal to his own faith, there can be discovered definite traces of a movement towards spiritual unification in the face of secular challenge; for example, there is the publication of *Thus we are Men*, which is an anthology of the beliefs of Christianity, Buddhism, Hinduism, Islam and Judaism. Ashby's formula of 'co-operation without compromise' is perhaps as near an alliance as the Traditional Creeds can ever achieve. The wistful lines of a poet which she heads with the remark of a seventeenth-century fellow-artist can best express the twentieth century's image of its absconded deity:

Deus Absconditus

'. . . so shall we be drawn by that sight from Ignorance and Sin. . . . But by what cords? The cords of a man, and the cords of Love.'

THOMAS TRAHERNE

'I selfish and forsaken do still long for you
God for whom I was born and should have died:
Like lovers over miles and miles of sea
I lean my heart toward my comfort uselessly;
Did man or God weep out this sundering tide?

Cut off each sense, withdraw to the inmost secret place:
This God absconds from every promised land.
To shrink like a mollusc and to find no grace
This is the lot his lovers face.

And yet the worst is, not to seek you; yet the worst
Is not to know our lack of you. O, Love,
By what cords will you draw us? As at first
The cords of a man? Not splendour but the penal flesh
Taken for love, that moves us most.

Who breaks his tryst in a passionate ritual
May burn in a dry tree, a cold poem,
In the weak limbs of a child, so instant and perpetual,
In the stranger's face of a father dying,
Tender still but all the while departing.

Here he is endured, here he is adored.
And anywhere. Yet it is a long pursuit,
Carrying the junk and treasure of an ancient creed,
To a love who keeps his faith by seeming mute
And deaf, and dead indeed.'

ANN RIDLER

REFERENCES

1. KIERKEGAARD, S.: *Journals* (Collins, 1958).*
2. MARCEL, G.: *An Essay in Autobiography* (Collins & Harvill, 1947).
3. See MARCEL, G.: *Man Against Humanity* (Harvill Press, 1952).*
4. MARCEL, G.: *On the Ontological Mystery* (1933).
5. MARCEL, G.: *Homo Viator* (Gollancz, 1957).
6. See *Three Plays* (Secker & Warburg, 1952) to which this lecture forms an introduction.*
7. BONHOEFFER, D.: *Letters and Papers from Prison* (SCM press revised edition, 1967).*
8. GUILLAUME, A.: *Islam* (Cassell, 1962), p. 192.*
9. SUZUKI, D. T.: *An Introduction to Zen Buddhism* (Arrow Books, 1959), from the foreword by Christmas Humphreys.*
10. SUZUKI, D. T.: *Mysticism, Christian and Buddhist* (Allen & Unwin, 1957), p. 37.*
11. WATTS, A. W.: op. cit.
12. op. cit.
13. See JUNG, C. G.: *Psychology and Religion: Collected Works*, Vol. 2— Foreword to the *I Ching* (Routledge, 1957).*
14. See Chapter V.
15. op. cit.
16. ASHBY, PHILIP, H.: *The Conflict of Religions* (New York, Scribners', 1955).

CHAPTER THREE

The State as God

'National Socialist Germany "gave up political liberty for psychic freedom".'

(WILSON KNIGHT, *Christ and Nietzsche*)

THROUGHOUT the previous chapter constant reference was made to the forces of nationalism, socialism and secularism as corroding the popular forms of the traditional faiths and inclining some of the professional defenders of them to reformulate their teachings. It is time now to scrutinize these forces more closely, recognizing that for large numbers, probably a majority of the world's population, their appeal has been and continues to be far more potent than any religious appeal and therefore of more effect in the working out of contemporary history. As Lewis Mumford points out in his book *The Condition of Man*:

'When religion ceased to be a political force politics became a substitute religion.'

Even more pointedly and with particular reference to our subsequent consideration of the totalitarianism of the Right and the Left, Talmon, in his book *Political Messianism: The Romantic Phase*, has commented on the religious and political interchange:

'. . . it was the seeming insouciance about ultimate ends and the pragmatic temper which repelled the Messianic Left (as well as the Right) in bourgeois liberals most. The latter appeared smug and selfish to seekers after the Absolute.'

Although secularism is no doubt the dominant feature of the nationalism, fascism, nazism and communism now to be examined, the fact should not be overlooked that in some instances, Aden and Pakistan, for example, the religious motivation is still active.

I. NATIONALISM

Volumes have been written about the meaning of nationalism[1], but a definition of it provided by John Stuart Mill in 1861 is probably the most serviceable here as indicating the kind of material out of which belief is woven:

> 'A portion of mankind may be said to constitute a Nationality if they are united among themselves by common sympathies which do not exist between them and any others—which make them co-operate with each other more willingly than with other people, desire to be under the same Government, and desire that it should be Government by themselves or a portion of themselves exclusively.'

It was at the end of the First World War that nationalism as thus defined in the sense of self-determination received a gigantic impulse forwards, which has by no means spent itself today. A positive rash of nation states has spread across the face of the world during the last fifty years, the result presumably of the tremendous pressure exercised by believers in nationalism. Examples spring readily to mind: Beneš and Masaryk for Czechoslovakia; the Army Nationalism of Japan; in China, first under Chiang Kai-shek, and later taking the form of National Communism under Mao Tse-tung; in India under Gandhi and Nehru; in Africa under men like Nkrumah and Nyerere. Two beliefs are common to all these movements, one the determination by a recognizable group to achieve responsibility for the conduct of its own affairs, the other an absolute determination by the non-European powers to shake off any kind of colonial domination. Permeating both of these beliefs, though in different forms and with different degrees of intensity, there was a third belief, namely an intense conviction that the time had come in the world's history for the common man to rise up and demand and procure mass social justice. (See Henderson and Caldwell, *The Chainless Mind*[2] for a specific treatment of these events.)

> '. . . it was the acceptance of the doctrine of a national personality, of an identification of all the people within the territory with the individuality of the State, of a belief in a kind of mystic brotherhood of the people that constituted the nation . . .

(And) if nationalism developed directly by resistance and indirectly by the recovery of historical sense and pride in cultural achievement as a result of western contact, the sense of Asianism is exclusively the counterpart of the solidarity of European feeling.'[3]

'. . . Nationalism had become the dominant political and cultural force among all the races and civilizations on earth.'[4]

Enough has been said to make the point that if by religion is meant 'that which concerns man ultimately' (Paul Tillich) then nationalism has become the religion of most of mankind over the last fifty years—not because it answers ultimate questions but because it provides possibly attainable satisfactions for basic human needs—food, clothing, housing and crude justice—which must always come before any real concern for final questions: these *are* most men's final questions. The tragic irony of this fact is that, due to huge population increases and the controls being achieved over disease, the very achievement of these basic needs under the banner of nationalism is being seriously threatened— the gap between 'haves' and 'have-nots' widens instead of narrowing; and what is the result? Surely it is that, in their frustration and despair, nationalist believers either become more extreme and fanatic than ever before or experiment with new forms of socio-political organization, mostly of a totalitarian kind—a theme which will be taken up again at the end of this chapter.

2. FASCISM

The sheer absurdity of the following extract from a Victorian Nursery Primer entitled *Near Home, or Europe Described* provides an amusing example of British insularity and its stereotype of, in this case, the Italians, who because they were neither British nor Protestant deservedly suffered Divine disapproval:

Question: What is the religion of the Italians?
Answer: They are Roman Catholics.
Question: What do the Roman Catholics worship?
Answer: Idols and a piece of bread.
Question: Would not God be very angry if He knew that the Italians worshipped idols and a piece of bread?
Answer: God *is* very angry.

It is only a short step from this kind of foolishness to the Englishman's statement of the late 1920's that Fascism was a good thing because it had made the Italian trains run on time. Behind this frivolity lies the sinister fact that the first totalitarianism of the Right occurred in Italy as a result of the seizure of power by Mussolini in 1922.

'All Fascist movements combine, I suggest, in varying proportions, a reactionary ideology and a modern mass organization. Their leaders, with no opposition, extol traditional values but they appeal for support to the masses and exploit any form of mass discontent that is available. In their original ideas they often closely resemble old-fashioned Conservatism, but their methods of struggle, indeed their whole notion of political organization belong not to the idealised past but to the modern age. Their outlook may be nostalgic and it is certainly élitist, but as a political force they are more democratic than oligarchic. The study of Fascism requires an understanding both of nineteenth-century European Conservatism and of the social conflicts within both the advanced industrial and the underdeveloped economies which co-existed in Europe between the world wars.'[5]

It is significant that this occurred in a traditionally Roman Catholic country in the centre of which lay the Papacy itself. What had happened to this particular brand of Christian religious belief to make the overwhelming majority of Italians neglect that allegiance for Fascist Nationalism? The reason is threefold. Politically Italy had emerged from the First World War with discredit. Economically she was suffering from the typical ills, unemployment included, of rapid urbanization and industrialization, with an attendant depreciation of agriculture, especially in the South. Psychologically many Italians were feeling the need more for a father of their country than a father in Heaven. Nurtured by D'Annunzio, the myth of the heroic 'dare-man' caught hold of people and made them ready to believe in a leader, like Mussolini, who promised them materially improved living conditions, a glamorous foreign policy and above all a sense of shared collective identity. In short, Fascism seemed to offer Italians an opportunity for integrating their lives emotionally and intellectually within the corporate state. A typical utterance of Mussolini confirms this idea:

'Fascism is the purest form of democracy if the nation be conceived . . . as the most powerful idea which acts within the nation.'

Mussolini's regime brought some short-term benefits with it such as an improved domestic efficiency and successful adventure abroad in the shape of the conquest of Abyssinia. In the long run it spelt catastrophe: Ignazio Silone has described in his moving novel *The Seed Beneath the Snow* how another type of belief did persist throughout the period of oppression, compounded partly of a purified and chastened Christianity and partly of a socialism unseduced by the specious arguments of the Fascists that they alone could give expression to proper and legitimate national feelings.

A clue worth taking up here is the fact that Fascism in Italy and Nazism in Germany both occurred in countries which were suffering from retarded and/or frustrated nationalism at a time when the Christian religion, Roman Catholic and Protestant, was beginning to lose its grip on the mass of the people—themselves just beginning to enjoy the fruits of some years of compulsory primary education. It seems as though people needed to believe that this considerable dislocation or at least rearrangement of their society contained a meaning for them, that traditional religion did not and could not express it but that the modern power state would. For this they were prepared to make sacrifices gladly and for many years without resentment: somehow 'it made them tick'.

3. NAZISM

Ten years after Fascism came to Italy Nazism came to Germany and for many of the same reasons, but this second totalitarianism of the Right proved to be far more formidable than the first. Geographic, demographic and psychological reasons were responsible for this. What in the 'twenties had not been much more than a local phenomenon had by the 'thirties and in the context of the world financial crisis of 1929 become a phenomenon of world significance. As Ernst Toller once remarked, 'When a man loses his power to believe, he takes opiates' (*Letters from Prison*). Hitler administered the most colossal opiate of all times to willing patients eager to become 'true believers' (see Hoffer, *The True Believers*).

The Hitler phenomenon provides the most considerable and telling evidence of the truth of our central thesis, namely that man demands to believe in ultimate things and that if he cannot use the traditional religious channels for the expression of them he will ruthlessly seize upon others. Jung in his *Essays on Contemporary Events* drew attention to the existence in Germany in the middle 1930's of the so-called 'German Faith Movement' which avowedly aimed at the religious renaissance of the nature and the hereditary foundation of the German race.

> 'One should compare this movement (a nominally Christian one) with the sermon preached by Dr. Langman, an evangelical clergyman and dignitary of the Church, at the funeral of the late Gustloff. Dr. Langman gave the address in S.A. uniform and top boots. He sped the deceased on his journey to Hades and directed him to Valhalla, to the home of Siegfried and Baldur, the heroes who are feeding the life of the German people by the sacrifice of their blood, like Christ among others. May this God send the people of the earth clanking their way through history.'[6]

One quotation from Alan Bullock's classic work *Hitler: A Study in Tyranny* suffices to clinch this point, namely that it was his extraordinary personality which found correspondence in the German people's need to experience integration in their domestic affairs and in the eyes of the rest of the world.

> 'Luck and the disunity of his opponents will account for much of Hitler's success—as it will of Napoleon's—but not for all. He began with few advantages, a man without a name and without support other than that which he acquired for himself, not even a citizen of the country he aspired to rule. To achieve what he did Hitler needed—and possessed—talents out of the ordinary which in sum amounted to political genius, however evil its fruits. Hitler indeed was a European no less than a

German phenomenon. The conditions and the state of mind which he exploited, the malaise of which he was the symptom, were not confined to one country although they were more strongly marked in Germany than anywhere else. Hitler's idiom was German, but the thoughts and emotions to which he gave expression have a more universal currency.'[4]

Thoughts and emotions 'of more universal currency' are the essential ingredients of these 'isms' of belief which are the substitute religions of our period. They mobilize the instinctive unconscious forces in the human psyche which, because they have failed to find outlet through the traditional channels of religions, force their way through new and socially disruptive ones.

4. COMMUNISM

In turning to consider our fourth 'ism', the greatest possible care must be taken to distinguish it from the totalitarianisms of the Right. For one thing they were defeated, while Communism continues its victories, but, even more important, Communism has become associated with young and vigorous nationalism and is itself based on 'a critique of political economy' (Karl Marx) which however open to formidable criticism has already left an irremovable stamp on many of the emerging societies of the twentieth century world.

Communism is a political philosophy and a political programme originating with Karl Marx, not inappropriately described by John Middleton Murray in his book *Heaven and Earth* as the last of the Medieval Schoolmen—a mighty prophet of our times. The Russian Revolution of 1917 was the application of Communist principles; Leninism was its development, modification and perversion; Stalinism was its consolidation in the face of threats from without; its incidence in parts of the world as remote from one another as China, Cuba, Yugoslavia and some of the African states proclaim its global relevance. The French historian Michelet remarked of the emergence of the nation state, 'le nouveau Messie est le Roi'; today it is tempting to recoin his phrase and say, 'le nouveau Messie est le Commissar'. (See Arthur Koestler's book *The Yogi and the Commissar*.)

What, then, is the essence of Communist belief? A conviction that the Marxist-Leninist interpretation of history makes sense of the human story in terms of class struggle: that all men are necessarily caught up in this pre-determined process of social evolution; that socialism and then communism are its inevitable final stage, the antithesis of capitalism; that the workers of the world are the fated instruments of this revolutionary achievement which gives them a total global solidarity. Communism is, as Carew Hunt puts it in his book *Theory and Practice of Communism*, 'a body of ideas which has filled the vacuum created by the breakdown of organized religion as a result of the increasing secularization of thought during the last three centuries'. This would seem to be particularly true of Russia with the virtual deification of Lenin. Carew Hunt comments on the ceremony following Lenin's death in 1924:

> 'The ceremony was calculated to stir the minds of a primitive semi-oriental people into a mood of exultation for the new Leninist cult. So was the mausoleum in the Red Square, in which Lenin's embalmed body was deposited, in spite of his widow's protest and the indignation of many Bolshevik intellectuals. To myriads of peasants whose religious instincts were repressed in the Revolution the mausoleum soon became a place of pilgrimage, the queer Mecca of an atheistic creed which needed prophets and saints and a holy sepulchre and icons.'

Again, as Edmund Wilson points out in his book *To the Finland Station*, 'the Dialectic then is a religious myth disencumbered of divine personality and tied up with the history of mankind'. To this, of course, it can be objected that if the Dialectic is a universal and eternal law, there is no reason why it should stop with Communism. To the ideological claim of Communism it can be objected that in fact recent history has provided examples of national, political expediency taking precedence over the correct Party Line. Yet none of this has undermined the belief of millions of men and women that Communism is the creed of the underdog and the oppressed—a passionate faith that it can bring them a social justice never before attempted in the history of man and that strong State action, if necessary assuming totalitarian dimensions, is not too high a price to pay for this tremendous prospect. 'Power to the Soviets, Land to the Peasants, Bread to the Starving and Peace to all men'; however tarnished, this watchword of Lenin can still work magic with the under-privileged and oppressed. It is especially connected, though in this way it is no different from other forms of sophisticated modern societies, with the conviction that through science man can mould his environment entirely, that nature has now become his creature: possibly the most dangerous of all the myths of the twentieth century as we shall see in our final chapter.

Professor Sir Isaiah Berlin in his excellent book, *Karl Marx* has caught the spirit and colossal significance of this fourth ism of belief.

'Marxism set out to refute the proposition that ideas govern the course of history. But the very extent of its own influence on human affairs has weakened the force of its thesis. For in altering the hitherto prevailing view of the relation of the individual to his environment and to his fellows, it has palpably altered the relation itself: and in consequence remains the most powerful among the intellectual forces which are today permanently transforming the ways in which men think and act.'[8]

Yet it too has its dark and sinister side as will become apparent when we now in the final section of this chapter attempt some psychological analysis of the phenomena of totalitarianism and their relation to democracy.

5. TOTALITARIANISM

The connecting thread in our exposition of the isms of belief has been the contention that they have come into existence, in some degree at least, as substitutes for the traditional religions. Their similarities and, even more, the differences between them have been noted: yet the fact that they share two characteristics is important. One is that they deal with the problem of evil either by ignoring or denying it or by the crude and effective method of simply projecting it on to real or imagined enemies, for example, in the case of the Nazis the use of the Jews as scapegoats, in the case of the Communists, the capitalists. The second is that they

deal with the problem of death either by ignoring it or by present-
ing it in the form of a kind of glorious sacrifice made by the young
and vigorous for their particular cause, nationalist or ideological,
to be suffered by the elderly and diseased as the price of their
social uselessness. In neither case is human personality believed
to be more than the sum of its two parts, body and ego, both
liable to damage while alive and destined to final annihilation
when dead. Any form of eschatological belief must by definition,
therefore, be a this-worldly one, and the experience of wholeness
and purpose for which human nature craves is to be achieved in
some kind of merging of the individual with the collective: hence
the explanation and justification of the totalitarian state. We shall
be taking up the question of recent and contemporary belief regarding evil and death again, but here it remains to probe a little
more deeply into the nature of totalitarianism.

Briefly stated, our proposition is that totalitarianism is the
response to man's demands for the experience of wholeness in an
age when the traditional religious faiths are inadequate to meet
it. The fact that this wholeness must logically embrace the dark
as well as the light, evil as well as good, explains the inevitable
presence of the daemonic element in all totalitarian phenomena,
however diverse their ideological premises: concentration camps
produce the same evils whether located in Siberia or Auschwitz.
Eloquent case histories exist to illustrate this theme, Pasternak's
Doctor Zhivago for Communist Russia, Thomas Mann's *Dr.
Faustus* for Nazi Germany. Indeed, through Dostoievsky's *The
Possessed* and Goethe's *Faust*, the whole problem of man's shadow
side can be studied; and it goes further back than this, of course,
into the natural history of the devil, but more of that later. Let
us merely note, in passing, Shigalov's remark in *The Possessed*,
'starting from a limited freedom I arrive at unlimited despotism'.
By analogy we could place alongside this: starting from the
Communist Manifesto we arrive at Stalin; starting from the
Weimar Republic we arrive at the Third Reich.

What belief, then, can withstand the giant strength of the
totalitarian claim? The answer was partly given by the allied
victory in the Second World War—the belief in democracy and
its will to resist totalitarianism; but such resistance could only
be made at a price, the most expensive part of which was democracy's own use of totalitarian weapons in war: Hiroshima followed

Dachau, and since 1945 the whole world has remained locked in a struggle between the democracies and the totalitarianisms (now chiefly Communist) with belief in the 'deterrent' being as yet only faintly balanced by belief in anything else, by belief in what Marcel has called 'a recourse to the transcendent' (see below).

It is necessary to distinguish clearly between totalitarianism and the various kinds of authoritarian dictatorship which have existed from time to time in history. The former is a recent phenomenon of essentially European origin. Firstly it is the expression of the unsolved problem of evil and death both in individual and collective terms; it is secondly the expression of what Ortega y Gasset calls 'the rise to power of the pseudo-educated masses' (*The Revolt of the Masses*); it is thirdly the concomitant of rapid industrialization and urbanization of previously rural communities. It is when a society has failed to come to terms with its political, economic and pyschological condition, after its ruling class has been implicated in this failure, that totalitarianism establishes itself. It expresses the reaction of large social groups away from the proposed as yet excessive challenge of democratic responsibility, either in a maladjusted society like Italy of the 1920's or an adolescent one like Ghana of the 1960's and back to dependence on authority figures. These are then endowed with the attributes of parental and shadow archetypes, which control the movements of the group from the depths of the unconscious. As Ernst Toller once put it, 'the desire for a dictator is the desire for castration'. This is the same as the desire for Big Brother, who, in an Orwellian nightmare paradise, caters for man's surrender of his individual virility.

By its nature totalitarianism establishes itself only when the political, economic and psycho-spiritual condition of society is of such a kind as to invite it. Once established, with all the equipment of modern power at its disposal, a totalitarian government cannot be resisted effectively from within by any of the traditional methods of conspiracy. If it is overthrown from without by alien conquest, its essential ingredients are not destroyed but driven underground. Resistance is beside the mark unless the instruments of that resistance themselves partake of the mystique in a positive sense of which totalitarianism is the daemonic shadow side.

At this point Marcel's reflections become truly relevant:

'But let us imagine, then, the state of our own country immediately after a Putsch or coup d'état: if rebellion is futile and a retreat into insignificance impracticable, what, supposing that we are fully aware of our situation, does there remain for us to do? At the risk of discontenting and even shocking those who still tend to think of solutions for political problems in terms of positive action, I shall say that in that region all the ways of escape seem to be barred. Our only recourse can be to the Transcendent: but what does that mean? The Transcendent, Transcendence? These are words which among philosophers and intellectuals, for a good many years past, have been strangely misused. When I myself speak here of a recourse to the Transcendent, I mean, as concretely as possible, that our only chance in the sort of horrible situation I have imagined is to appeal, I should perhaps not say to a power, but rather to the level of being, an order of the spirit, which is also the level of grace, of mercy, of charity; and to proclaim, while there is still time, that is to say before the State's psychological manipulations have produced in us the alienation from our true selves that we fear, that we repudiate in advance the deeds and the acts that may be obtained from us by any sort of constraint whatsoever. We solemnly affirm, by this appeal to the Transcendent, that the reality of ourselves lies beyond any such acts and any such words. . . . What we have to do is to proclaim that we do not belong entirely to the world of objects and to which men are seeking to assimilate us, in which they are straining to imprison us. To put it very concretely indeed, we have to proclaim that this life of ours, which it has now become technically possible to make into a grimacing parody of all our dreams, may in reality be only the more insignificant aspect of a grand process unfolding itself far beyond the boundaries of the visible world. In other words, this means to say that all philosophies of Immanence have had their day, that in our own day they have revealed their basic unreality or, what is infinitely more serious, their complicity with these modern idolatries which it is our duty to denounce without pity; the idolatry of race, the idolatry of class . . . a man cannot be free or remain free, except in the degree to which he remains linked with that which transcends him, whatever the particular form of the link may be, for it is pretty obvious that the form of the link need not reduce itself to official and canonical prayers. . . .

'It can never be too strongly emphasized that the crisis which Western man is undergoing today is a metaphysical one: there is probably no more dangerous illusion than that of imagining that some readjustment of social conditions could suffice of itself to appease a contemporary sense of disquiet, which rises in fact from the very depths of man's being.'[9]

With this profound declaration of belief, the tenability of which we shall be considering in the course of our final chapter, we must finish our first survey of the isms of belief. Let us hope that sufficient has been said to indicate why they have been so compelling and yet why they are so inadequate.

REFERENCES

1. See KOHN, HANS: *The Idea of Nationalism* (Macmillan, 1961).*
2. HENDERSON, J. L. & CALDWELL, M.: *The Chainless Mind* (Hamish Hamilton, 1968).
3. PANIKKAR: *Asia and Western Dominance* (Allen & Unwin), pp. 331–2.
4. KOHN, H.: op. cit., p. 89.
5. SETON WATSON, HUGH: 'Fascism, Right and Left', *Journal of Contemporary History, International Fascism, 1920–1945*, Vol. 1, No. 1, 1966.
6. JUNG, C. G.: *Essays on Contemporary Events* (Kegan Paul, 1947).
7. BULLOCK, ALAN: *Hitler: A Study in Tyranny* (Odhams), pp. 735 et seq.*
8. BERLIN, I.: *Karl Marx* (Home University Library), p. 174.*
9. MARCEL, G.: *Man Against Humanity* (Harvill Press, 1952), pp. 17 et seq.*

CHAPTER FOUR

Alternative Panaceas

'The truth is that science has developed a conception of hard, sober, intellectual strength that makes mankind's old metaphysical and moral notions simply unendurable, although all it can put in their place is the hope that a day, still distant, will come when a race of intellectual conquerors will descend into the valleys of spiritual fruitfulness.' (Robert Musil *The Man without Qualities*, Vol. 1, p. 48.)

I. SCIENCE

Pervading all the isms of belief there has been one which predominates, namely belief in science, the almost automatic assumption, which crept into popular thought after the end of the nineteenth century, that the key of scientific method would sooner or later open the door to everything, that the 'inexplicable was only the unexplained'. Typical of this attitude, and one common to such ideologically opposed societies as the Soviet Union and the U.S.A., was the conviction that there was no problem which could not be solved if not today then tomorrow. This outlook was a direct outcome of the triumph of Renaissance man, aptly illustrated in the Faust story and culminating in our own day in a slavish worship of information for information's sake, and divorced from any scale of values.

In a series of B.B.C. talks entitled *Faust's Damnation: The Morality of Knowledge*, and later in his book *The Artist's Journey to the Interior*, Professor Erich Heller has elaborated this theme with scholarly and profound insight:

'He (the modern Piccolo Faust) is so unsure of what ought to be known that he has come to embrace a preposterous superstition: everything that can be known is also *worth* knowing:

178

including the more manifestly worthless. Already we are unable to see the wood for the trees of knowledge; or the jungle either. Galley slaves of the free mind, aimlessly voyaging, we mistake our unrestrainable curiosity, the alarming symptom of spiritual tedium, for scientific passion. Most of that which flourishes in these days as "science", said Kierkegaard, is not science but indiscretion, and he and Nietzsche said that the natural sciences will engineer our destruction. . . . If once Dr. Faustus has sold his soul to the Devil for the promise of success in his search for Truth he now tries to annul the bargain by turning scientist and insisting that in his role as a Searcher for Truth he has no soul. Yet the Devil was not to be cheated. When the time came, he proved that the search, conducted behind the back of the soul, had led to a Truth that was Hell. . . . The black magic of Faust is the poetically fantastic rendering of Goethe's belief that evil arises from any knowing and doing of man that is in excess of his being.'[1]

Before going on to make the obvious connection between this diagnosis of the negative aspect of science and the emergence of Existentialism, it would be as misleading as it would be wrong not to remind ourselves of the great and glorious, positive aspect of science, on the achievements of which most of modern civilization is based. To this we shall return in our final chapter, but the point to be established here is that a belief in what is in fact an out of date, materialistic (in the nineteenth-century sense of that word) concept of science has come to form the core of a secularism consisting in an idolatry of things, admirably depicted in the Proustian world of Time Lost.

2. EXISTENTIALISM

This is a religious and philosophical movement of the last hundred years. Although it has become very much a two-fold response, religious and secular, to the twentieth-century world scene, its point of departure was the work of the great Danish thinker, Søren Kierkegaard. The despair which his young man of 1851 reveals when he exclaims: 'I stick my finger into existence—it smells of nothing', was the prophetic anticipation of 'I couldn't care less.' Existentialism is the attempt to wrest a meaning from existence either by a transcendence of the conventional religious categories or by a denial of them and by a kind of affirmation—in in spite of it all—of transitory human life. In other words, existentialism is an actor not a spectator philosophy of life—it points to a way of life—it seeks a way of coping with that feeling of 'alienation' from any meaningful reality which seems to attend so many of us to-day.

As H. J. Blackham says in his book *Six Existentialist Thinkers*:

'It appears to be reaffirming in a modern idiom the protestant or stoic form of individualism which stands over against the empirical individualism of the Renaissance or of modern liberalism or of Epicurus as well as over against the universal system of Rome or of Moscow or of Plato.'[2]

'What the Existentialist implies about man is that he, alone among other beings, is a decision-making creature, blessed, or cursed, with the freedom to choose among a variety of possibilities in an absurd and mysterious existence; to be truly human, man must accept this freedom and conquer the anxiety and despair that threaten it by "commitment" to a way of life. This message can be bracing, notably in the religious version of Existentialism in which the commitment is directed towards a spiritual goal. It can also be nihilistic, notably in the atheistic version, in which commitment is demanded for its own sake only and the despair of the human situation is emphasized more than its conquest. Both movements, the logicians as well as the lotus-eaters, appear to do away with what has usually been considered the very heart of philosophy—metaphysics, the attempt to comprehend through reason the nature of reality.'[3]

The chief figures in existentialist thought have been Marcel and Jaspers on the religious side, Heidegger partly, Sartre and Camus wholly on the secular side.

MARCEL draws attention by means of his philosophical essays and his plays to a profound distinction between a problem and a mystery, the latter being 'a problem which encroaches on its own data'.[4]

JASPERS: '. . . tries to show how even in face of the shipwreck of all earthly hopes and ideals man can still affirm his relationship to the Transcendent. He offers us a religious philosophy, but at the same time a post-Christian religious philosophy.'[5]

HEIDEGGER: '... is engaged in ontological enquiry and analysis on an academic basis, but the Heidegger who has exercised the most influence is without a doubt the philosopher who describes man as 'thrown' into the world and as faced with the choice between authentic and unauthentic existence in a world from which God is declared to be "absent".'[6]

SARTRE, as philosopher, novelist and playwright, remarks and explains: 'Hell is other people'—'the metaphysical malady of being bored' is what is the matter with us; phrases like these are clues to such works of his as La Nausée and Huis Clos. Like many other artists of this century Sartre is obsessed with the notion of time as a prison from which there is no escape. It is what Malraux calls 'the metallic realm of the Absurd'—the human predicament which Buber from quite a different point of view described as being constituted of 'Existential Reciprocal Mistrust'. For a penetrating psychological analysis of this condition see R. D. Laing's The Divided Self (Penguin, 1959).

CAMUS was always testing out his knowing in what he did and what he was. (See Henderson & Caldwell, The Chainless Mind.) How could modern man escape the fate of being either victim of executioner in domestic and foreign arenas of violence? 'I rebel and therefore we exist', he pronounced boldly, and his novels and note-books are moving testimony to his constant search for an escape from the dilemma he posited:

'Can one be a Saint without God? That is the problem.'

(The Plague)

'Real generosity towards the future lies in giving all to the present.'

(The Rebel)

Of both theistic and atheistic existentialists it may be said 'modern man, alienated from his true self, strives to find it. Philosophy can illuminate his way. But the last word remains with man's liberty. Philosophy can illuminate choice, it cannot perform a man's act of choice for him.'[7]

3. PACIFISM

The essence of Pacifism, of which there are numerous versions, consists in the belief that it is wrong to employ violence in settling disputes and especially so by resorting to war. Two strains in it can be clearly discerned, the spiritual-moral and the political-utilitarian, and frequently they mingle with each other. In the twentieth century there have been two instances of Pacifism at work and there is a third form of it possibly looming.

First there is the pacifism which, especially in Great Britain, arose from revulsion at the horrors of the First World War. In a few other European countries and in the U.S.A. this continued during the 1920's and early 1930's in the shape of 'NO MORE WAR' movements. One element was that of Christian Pacifism, another that of neo-Marxist Socialism, the third a kind of over-naïve faith that both in political as well as in individual relations decency must prevail if only the other cheek is turned with sufficient consistency. The rise and onslaught of the dictatorships wrecked these hopes, and Pacifism as a European phenomenon was swallowed up by the Second World War. Nevertheless the distinguished examples of Pacifist witness, such as that of the relief work of the Society of Friends and the Pacifist martyrs of some of the Resistance Movements, should not be forgotten. This type of Pacifism was a not ignoble but somewhat pathetic blend of spiritual idealism and political *Realpolitik*, weakest in its inadequately conceived image of the springs of human personality.

Secondly there is the Pacifism of Mahatma Gandhi and the non-violent resistance to British rule in India culminating in that country's independence in 1947. Here, of course, the ingredients were different: Hindu and Buddhist teachings, the idea of *Ahimsa* or harmlessness, and above all the principle and practice of *Satyagraha*—the positive force of non-violence as a technique for overcoming enemies. The very measure of its comparative success in this particular case, where, to some degree at least, Indian and British decencies responded to and respected one another, deceived many into believing that here was a universal panacea. They either could not or would not perceive the very high price in human self-discipline and readiness to suffer the retaliation from others which such a stance demands. Since Gandhi's assassination, and in spite of the devoted pilgrimages of

Vinoba Bhave, India under Nehru and his successors has rejected the way of pacifism as a political policy. This has led to chagrin and disillusionment among many non-Indians who tended to regard Gandhi's India as others had regarded the young Soviet Union, as the light of the world, and who were bitterly disappointed when that light flickered and apparently failed.

However, during the last twenty years, with the advent of nuclear weapons and the horrific stalemate of the deterrent policy, not to mention the unspeakable horrors of such war as is waged, for example, in Vietnam, there has been a revival of interest in Pacifism, partly as a tenable moral position and partly as a sensible political expedient. It seems to be taking two forms: on the one hand it seeks to discover where and what in human personality is the element that can preserve its integrity and survive even when exposed to the extremes of the most refined methods of modern oppression and torture: on the other it is exploring the nature of conflict in general and war in particular by playing 'war games'. The object of these is to subordinate war-inclining situations to scientific control of the elements which determine them. In a world where war has become genocide it may well be that belief in a reformed pacifism makes good sense.[8]

4. SPIRITUALISM

The most extraordinary single fact about human existence is that no one knows what it is. That is why, throughout history, Spiritualism in one form or another has persisted. To distinguish it from what in our own times has become the science of psychical research (see Chapter V), Spiritualism is here taken to mean belief of an emotive and inspirational kind in the possibility of communication between the living and the dead. In its modern form, spiritualism is almost entirely a western phenomenon and in that context it has been looked at askance and often with downright condemnation by the Roman Catholic Church, while it has gained some distinct support from the Protestant denominations.

In his book *The Personality of Man*, G. N. M. Tyrrell correctly drew a sharp distinction between spiritualism and psychical research which, he says, 'is not superstition but a scientific study of human personality beyond the threshold of consciousness'.[9]

Spiritualism is not necessarily a mere superstition, but it is certainly a cult which claims thousands of devotees who believe that it is the grand truth which gives meaning to life. Gently ridiculed by Noel Coward in his play *Blithe Spirit*, its hold is tenacious, as is perfectly understandable because it ministers to the human hankering for personal survival after death. Its main features are crisply summarized in the following quotation:

'Spiritualists believe that the activity of human beings is not entirely limited to the use they make of their bodily or material organisms on this planet. It is held that those organisms were constructed by an animating principle which having entered into relation with matter for the purpose of developing an individuality can continue long after the temporary material body is worn out or otherwise resolved into its elements; and further, that the personalities thus brought into existence carry with them their memory, character, tastes and affections which they have developed here while in association with matter and should be able under certain limitations to guide and influence terrestrial affairs in cooperation with those still living on the earth.'

5. NEW MESSIANISM

Many millions of the world's population occupy positions midway between the beliefs of primitivism and the aspirations of modernism, secularist, scientific and nationalist. They are the subjects of the New Messianism, and their characteristics have already received classical study in Vittorio Lanternari's book *The Religion of the Oppressed—A Study of Modern Messianic Cults.* As that author points out:

'The Messianic movements of modern times constitute one of the most interesting and astonishing results of the cultural clash between populations in their different stages of development.'[10]

A great number of them had their first encounter with western civilization via the Christian Missionary Churches, and much, though by no means all, of the stuff of the national liberation movements of the twentieth century is imbued with the Christian religious and eschatological message. Another study indicates that the new Messianism may also be a kind of compensation for rejection of a few by a majority in a group—in this case the rejection of West Indians by whites.[11]

Lanternari's survey includes Nativistic Religious Movements in Africa, the Peyote Cult and other Prophetic Movements in North America, Religious Movements in Central and South America, and Messianic Movements in Melanesia, Polynesia, Asia and Indonesia.

Messianic cults 'involve a belief in Society's return to its source, they are expressed in terms of the expectation of the millennium and the cataclysms and catastrophes that are to precede it, and also embody a belief in the raising of the dead, in the reversal of the existing social order, in the ejection of the white man, in the end of the world, and in its regeneration in an age of abundance and happiness.'[12]

'. . . primitive societies have borrowed from the evangelism of the missionaries a great many elements in which they show a reflection of their own experience of life, even though portrayed in western Christian terms. This has occurred among such widely separated peoples as the Maoris of New Zealand and the Kikuyus of Kenya, the Bantus of South Africa, the Negroes of Jamaica and the Ghost Dance followers of North America. Here an indigenous population persecuted by its European rulers and familiar with the Bible has found in the ever-persecuted Jews a Biblical counterpoint of its own plight and because of this identification has felt inclined to claim direct descent from the tribes of Israel. The polygamy practised by David, Jacob and Solomon offered religious justification for the polygamy of the natives which the missionaries had so violently condemned. The messianic quest for escape from servitude took Moses for its model, and arrest, capture and death of a native prophet sought its inspiring precedent in the Passion of Jesus Christ. Certain aboriginal groups have found a validation of their traditional beliefs in such western messianic movements of Judeo-Christian derivation as Jehovah's Witnesses.'[13]

'This self-Christianization among native groups came about when the Whites, having forced their way into the native environment, created conditions similar to those which fostered the growth of early Christianity. As it was for the first Christians of the Middle East and of Ancient Rome, so it was for the native peoples of Africa, Asia, Oceania and the Americas: pressures and oppression came upon them simultaneously from two sides, the militant hierarchy of the Church and the authoritarian power of the State.'[14]

'The fact is that Christianity is being translated into pagan terms, instead of paganism being raised to the level of Christian values, for what appeals to the natives is not the spiritual significance of the doctrine but the magical power which they attribute to it. . . . What occurred among the New Guinea tribes of Markham Valley in 1941 at the outbreak of World War II offers a striking example of how artificial and devoid of roots the effects of missionary propaganda often are. The Missions in this area, being German Lutheran, were closed down when hostilities broke out, and their members were interned in Australia as Nazis. No sooner had this occurred than Pagan religious life sprang into the open revealing a tremendous vitality clandestinely nurtured for many a long year. This is what a native had to say about his own religious convictions: "If the missionaries asked us who made our crops grow, we told them it was as they said, God, who lived above, made them come up. But we knew it was not God. It was the magic we had performed that made the yams grow big. Food does not come up on its own, and if we stopped these things we would have nothing. We hid them and knew our gardens would be well." '[15]

'Pagan religious life springing into the open, revealing a tremendous vitality, clandestinely nurtured for many a long year'— these words evoke a curious resonance in the context expecially of Nazism as described in the previous chapter. It seems to point towards a law of global validity with local variations, to the effect that where the Absolute is not experienced consciously through socially acceptable channels, it will force its way with instinctive fury through channels of its own, long prepared by ancient need and custom.

6. RACISM

Finally there is what must quite categorically be described as the false belief of racism.[16] It is dealt with here rather than in the previous chapter because it falls into a different category from the 'isms' described there. The first point to grasp is that racism is a particular symptom of the general inability or unwillingness of human beings to tolerate differences among themselves—in this case the differences of skin colour and physiognomy. Although this is an age-old phenomenon, witness anti-semitism, it is not until this century that it has become a world-wide catastrophic one. Previously the encounters between groups of differently coloured peoples have been fitful and have nearly always taken the form of relationships between a powerful ruling minority and a weak, dependent majority, especially in the case of white and non-white in Asia and Africa. With the gaining of their national independence by dozens of countries and the tremendous increase in the speed of communication and interpenetration of cultures between peoples of all colours, this situation has changed completely. Nevertheless owing to the frequency and suddenness of these global encounters thousands more people are now aware of the differences between themselves and their neighbours, and this at the very time when most of them are experiencing the many dislocations and indeed agonies of modernization. In such a situation their need for scapegoats becomes irresistible, and so the use of that well-tried, if abominable psychological mechanism is invoked.

There is a peculiar irony in the fact that the scapegoat mechanism was most atrociously employed, not among the so-called underdeveloped people, but in Europe, in Germany which prided itself on being in the forefront of civilization. Much has been written to account for this, so we need do no more here than remind ourselves of the rationalization which accompanied this 'myth of the Twentieth Century', give one horrific example of it and spell out clearly the psychological implications of it. This may then be applied *mutatis mutandis* to the incidence of such racist belief in any part of the globe.

Rosenberg and Goebbels under the Hitler regime supplied with brutal thoroughness the notion attributable in part to Houston Stewart Chamberlain (*The Foundation of the Nineteenth*

Century, original German edition, 1899) of a superior Nordic
Aryan race to whom Destiny had decreed that all non-Aryans
and especially Jews should be subject. This false belief, erected
on an erroneous definition of the word Aryan and with no kind
of scientific justification whatsoever, spoke to the concern of the
unemployed and frustrated masses of German people in the dis-
credited Weimar Republic and offered them a daemonic messianic
alternative—all those who were not *Herrenvolk* could and should
be treated as *Untermenschen*—Sub-men, an inferior breed of
human beings, who must necessarily be eliminated if they could
not be profitably employed—this to apply with special force to
the enemy within their own gates, namely the Jews. That such a
programme could succeed must be attributed to the absence of
any counter-balancing belief of equal or greater force: that this
did not then and there exist, Chapters I and II have already
demonstrated. The result was that once the restraints of civilization and sophistication, themselves the fruits of careful spiritual
disciplining over a long period of time, were lifted, European
man showed himself as bestial and primitive as any other inhabi-
tant of the earth, with the added horror of up-to-date instruments
for expressing his bestiality. Books like Reitlinger's *The Final
Solution* and Alexander Donat's *The Holocaust Kingdom* have
told the story: the latter's description of the ghetto in Warsaw
and the Concentration Camp at Maidanek are essential knowledge for anyone presuming to try to make sense of the twentieth
century's human predicament. One Sartrian-like quotation must
suffice:

'. . . Maidanek was hell. Not the naïve inferno of Dante, but a
twentieth-century hell where the art of cruelty was refined to
perfection and every facility of modern technology and psychology was combined to destroy man physically and spiritually. . . . "This is a K. L.", said the Barrack Elder, "remember
those two initials, K. L. . . . Konzentrationslager. This is a
death camp, a Vernichtungslager. You have been brought here
to be destroyed by hunger, beating, hard labour and sickness.
You will be eaten by lice, you will rot in your own shit. Let me
give you one single piece of advice: forget who and what you
were. This is a jungle and here the only law is the law of the
strongest. No-one here is a Mr. Director or a Herr Doktor.

Everyone here is the same; everyone here is shit. All are going to die." '¹⁷

So much for one example of the result of a belief in racism. How, then, can such a thing come about? Books on the psychology of prejudice provide a plain answer: whenever social, economic and political conditions are conducive to a lowering of reasonably decent standards of human behaviour, men and women regress to a primitive instinctual level where the only way in which they can deal with their sense of inadequacy, weakness and guilt is by projecting it on to others: they need to believe in the black wickedness of what is most blatantly and apparently different from themselves, but what in fact corresponds most closely to themselves—the other race. No wonder Dr. Rees, then Director of the World Federation of Mental Health, remarked with regard to racial prejudice that 'it is, like malaria, an antisocial and killing disease. It comes in epidemics. Six million died of it in Germany. Two million in Pakistan.'

Now let us swing the searchlight of this illuminating diagnosis across the planet: what does it reveal? In almost every country some instance of racial intolerance and persecution: four main examples suggest themselves at once, Notting Hill and Smethwick in Great Britain, Newark and Detroit in U.S.A., Sharpeville in South Africa, Jerusalem's Wailing Wall in the Middle East. In simple, sober language we are forced to conclude this survey of some other human beliefs with the sad admission that the false one of racism commands the allegiance of millions and consists in the delusion that because other peoples' skins and physiognomies are not the same as their own they must be bad.

REFERENCES

1. HELLER, E.: *The Listener*, January 11, 1962.
2. BLACKMAN, H. J.: *Six Existentialist Thinkers* (Routledge & Kegan Paul, 1961), p. v of the paperback edition.
3. *Time Magazine*, January 7, 1966, 'What, if anything, to expect from today's philosophers'.
4. MARCEL, G.: op. cit.
5. COPLESTON, S. J., FREDERICK, C.: *Contemporary Philosophy;*

Studies of Logical Positivism and Existentialism (Burns & Oates, 1955).*

6. op. cit., p. 142.

7. op. cit., p. 174.

8. See SHARP, GENE: 'The Political Equivalent of War—Civilian Defence' in *International Conciliation*, November 1965 (No. 555), published by The Carnegie Endowment for International Peace; see also *Non-Violent Action—Theory and Practice*, a selected bibliography by APRIL CARTER, DAVID HOGGETT and ADAM ROBERTS, (Hausmann, 1966).

9. TYRRELL, G. N.: *The Personality of Man* (Pelican, 1958), p. 44.*

10. LANTERNARI, VITTORIO: *The Religion of the Oppressed—A Study of Modern Messianic Cults* (MacGibbon & Kee, 1963), p. 301.*

11. See CALLEY, M. J. C.: *God's People, West Indian Pentecostal Sects in England* (O.U.P., 1965).*

12. LANTERNARI: op. cit., p. 303.

13. op. cit., pp. 306–7.

14. op. cit., p. 315.

15. op. cit., pp. 317–19, and quoting READ, K. E.: 'Effects of the War on Markham Valley, New Guinea', *Oceania*, XVIII, 2 (1947), p. 114.

16. See SEGAL, R.: *The Race War* (Cape, 1966).*

17. DONAT, ALEXANDER: *The Holocaust Kingdom* (Secker & Warburg), pp. 167–8.*

CHAPTER FIVE

The Prospects of Belief

'Grant me intention, purpose and design
That's near enough for me to the Divine.'

(ROBERT FROST)

AGAINST the background of this survey of religious and secular belief in the twentieth century, we shall now attempt to evaluate its prospects. At the end of his essay on 'The Will to Believe'[1] William James poses the problem with stark simplicity:

'What do you think of yourself? What do you think of the world? These are riddles of the Sphinx, and in some way or other we must deal with them. If we decide to leave the riddles unanswered, that is a choice, but whatever choice, we make it at our peril. We stand on a mountain pass in the midst of whirling snow and blinding mist, through which we get glimpses now and then of paths which may be deceptive. If we stand still, we shall be frozen to death. If we take the wrong road, we shall be dashed to pieces. We do not certainly know that there is any right one.'

Our survey bears out the contention of Ortega y Gasset regarding the religious situation of modern man—'God, but in the background', and in that background there lurk many strange jungle beasts of a quite non-religious kind. Our survey has however raised with fearful urgency the question whether it is possible to 'build a traditionally solid house on a metaphysically condemned site?'[2] Surely the answer must be 'no' and the implication that we require a different kind of credal architecture and metaphysical basis. As long ago as 1928, Pierre Teilhard de Chardin affirmed 'an obscure faith in the march of Thought or

191

Spirit which is an insatiable power and destroys everything that has had its time'. In 1929, John Dewey wrote:

> 'The problem of restoring integration and cooperation between man's beliefs about the world in which he lives and his beliefs about the values and purposes that should direct his conduct is the deepest problem of modern life.'

In 1965 Philip Leon wrote a book with the significant title *Beyond Belief and Unbelief: Creative Nihilism*. It is aimed at what he calls 'the Ishmaelites or the Displaced Persons of the World of the Spirit'.[3] The rest of this book is written precisely from their point of view with the aim of describing the signposts, if any, which point towards a recovery of belief in the 'power of Spirit over things' beyond the previous religious and secular creeds. As will become apparent, this involves adopting finally a religious attitude, defined as one in which 'the individual accepts the burden of the incarnation of new values'.[4] This we must do, moreover, in that state of 'ontological insecurity' described by William James and clinically analysed by Laing in his book *The Divided Self*; but then, as that elegant spiritual warrior, Kierkegaard, reminds us:

> 'All religious (not to say Christian) adventure is on the further side of probability, is by letting go of probability.'

We may advance along three avenues, art, depth psychology and modern science. Art has already been reconnoitred in the first half of this book, but a few more words may help to confirm its thesis and justify still further the twin treatment of Art and Belief in one volume. For as Rilke stated in 1898, the artist is 'Eternity protruding into Time'. Aesthetics was once described as 'the science of sensuous knowledge' (Baumgarten, 1733) and as such cannot help being a useful indicator of what men and women believe, for all of us in varying degrees live through our senses. As has already been shown, modern Art in the western world is the outcome of a traceable and distinctive process. Following the argument in Sir Herbert Read's book *Icon and Idea*, it would appear that since the Renaissance western man began to suffer from a corruption of consciousness caused by the scientific compulsion (compare the Faust story) which tempted him to 'hold on to sensation so inevitably dissociating himself from it and becoming critical of it. The artist, that is to say, was content to give a deliberate illustration of intellectual concepts and religious dogmas that had never entered his consciousness as sensations or feelings, but were present to him as already received ideas, as lifeless formulas.'[5] Read explains how this process has in our own time reached a corrective climax:

'The post-Renaissance period should be regarded as one in which an infinite refinement of accepted symbols took place, and, with a parallel or consequent development, there was an infinite refinement of image and thought. But a time came when all that could be done had been done—refinement ended in sophistication, and little remained but repetition and return. But out of this very weariness and phantasy a new consciousness was to be born—the consciousness of the unconscious. A further attempt was made to circumvent all ideals, whether of God or of Man, and to present not the illusion of the real but the reality of consciousness—its subjective reality.'[6]

Do we not in the phrase 'a new consciousness came to be born' already descry on this avenue traces of that elusive new credal architecture and metaphysical base for which we are searching? Today's art surely reveals a 'cleavage between our mechanical and materialistic civilization and the aesthetic and spiritual values that consitute culture'. How far, we may next presume to wonder, can a growing consciousness of the unconscious, especially as portrayed in art, succeed in helping to remove the cleavage? The answer to this question is a very long way indeed, but this needs to be justified by an exploration of our second avenue of advance, namely the psychological one, with particular reference to the significance of the concept of the unconscious. While thus engaged we shall be taking up once again, as anticipated in Chapter II, the theme of current beliefs about evil and death.

*

The existence of the unconscious cannot be proved, but it has shown itself to be an almost, if not entirely, indispensable hypothesis for the exploration of certain phenomena not otherwise explicable. Since it was pioneered by Freud, Adler and Jung, their successors have offered a variety of interpretations of it, but we shall naturally employ the one that helps to make sense of our present concern, namely the prospect of a new human belief. It is based on depth psychology, chiefly of the Jungian kind, the best introductions to which are to be found in Frieda Fordham's book *Introduction to Jung* and P. W. Martin's *Experiment in Depth*.

The key idea is that of consciousness resting on and being derived from an individual and collective unconscious, between which there is a constant bi-polar and complementary relationship; all that which is in consciousness being by definition in the unconscious. Human personality can be pictured thus:

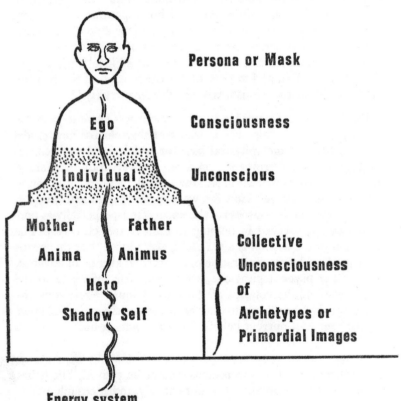

Persona or Mask

Consciousness

Unconscious

Collective
Unconsciousness
of
Archetypes or
Primordial Images

Energy system
constituted by
tension between opposites
of Conscious and Unconscious

On the basis of countless case studies, the proposition has been formulated that psychological growth consists in the process whereby a human being integrates what was previously unconscious into consciousness. The first stage of this is when the young child begins to speak of himself in the first instead of the third person—the birth of the ego, the second step, rarely attained until middle age, and often not even then, is when the centre of personality shifts from Ego—the centre of consciousness, to Self—the centre of total personality, conscious and unconscious. In all this the role of the archetypes is decisive—they are the energy-giving primordial images which, if conducted through appropriate symbols, promote the positive achievement of the process but which, if lacking proper symbolic conductors, can and do blow consciousness to smithereens. In individuals this latter phenomenon is called psychosis, in societies, chaotic anarchy. An apposite comment of Gerald Heard may be quoted here:

'If the Empire (Rome) died of pernicious anaemia, we are attacked not by that but by convulsions, by a social epilepsy.'[7]

The archetypes of the collective unconscious may be thought of as continually manifesting themselves in symbolic and conceptual forms on the time-track of an individual's span of existence between birth and death. Three main ones are pertinent to our present purpose. Just as the hero traditionally goes through the experiences of separation, initiation and return, so does each individual Ego. Like the hero of Myth, the Ego is either defeated and killed by the enemy, and that is the end of him—human death, or he kills the dragon and captures the princess or treasure which in psychological terms means the Self. Essential to the hero is his enemy, essential to the ego is its shadow without which the conflict of creation cannot take place. Here we come close to an essential stage of our argument, which may be crudely anticipated by saying that a regained belief in the value of evil and the meaning of death can be the outcome of a profound enough understanding of the implications of depth psychology.

'Evil', said Simone Weil, 'is the shadow of Good. All real Good, endowed with solidity and density, projects Evil. It is only imaginary Good which does not project Evil.'[8]

This reflection can lead us to consider the role of evil in human affairs and the nature of its personification in the Devil. It is perhaps helpful to conceive of his figure as originating in early man's projection of everything that he felt as threatening his sense of security and personal identity on to some external object or other person. As soon, in fact, as he became detached from his original identification and *Participation Mystique*⁹ man became aware of the perils of his new condition, as represented, for example, by the hazards of nature—'that devil of a wind'. Everything that was not himself had to be seen as his not-self, his opposite and as a most deadly enemy when it threatened to destroy his tender young ego: hence, animism and the need to propitiate the gods or devils: also the dualist mysteries of the Orient and the emergence of the figure of Satan—the semitic word meaning 'to oppose'. After a long and active career—the Council of Constantinople even declared him eternal in A.D. 574—he was apparently cut down to shape by the beginning of this century. In the 1910 edition of the *Encyclopaedia Britannica* (Vol. VIII, 'An Article on the Devil') the following appears:

'. . . it may be confidently affirmed that belief in Satan is not now generally regarded as an essential article of the Christian faith, nor is it found to be an indispensable element of Christian experience.'

Is this, one wonders, acceptable Christian doctrine today, and, if so, why? Denis de Rougemont in *The Devil's Share* (1944) invited us to consider whether the 'little gentleman' in Dostoievsky's novel *The Brothers Karamazov* is 'an objective reality or the projection of the unadmitted elements in his soul?' 'Well,' says the Devil in André Gide's *The Counterfeiters*, 'why are you scared of me? You know very well I don't exist.' 'The Devil's cleverest wile', wrote Baudelaire, 'is to convince us that he does not exist.'

It is, however, Jung, through his psychological approach, who has reinstated evil and the Devil, not as theological doctrines but as psychic realities. He has done so as a result of his examination of what he discovered empirically over and over again to be the 'inferior function' of human personality.

'I think it will help you to understand the term "Shadow",' he writes, 'if you consider first its relation to the Ego. Shadow implies that there is a source of light in front of your body which casts a shadow behind you. The source of light is consciousness.

Consciousness, like light, casts a shadow. Always that function which is behind you, depending where the light is, is in the shadow.'[10]

There is the personal, individual shadow of man's inferior function, consisting of that which the conscious position deprecates, his mortal enemy[11]—his *bête noire*—the side of himself which, when he recognizes it, he dislikes, and which is usually repressed but which is apt to erupt when its opposite in consciousness is too far stretched. There is also the archetypal shadow, an autonomous complex of the collective consciousness. It is through learning to recognize and accept shadow phenomena without surrendering to them that we can obtain access, as through a dark and dangerous gateway, to the unconscious and so eventually to the Self or core of human totality. 'Nobody is whole without negative qualities', said Jung, and life involves the coming to terms with that negative quality. What are its symptoms? It is a frequent element in dreams; it is a literary phenomenon, e.g. Caliban as Prospero's shadow—'This thing of darkness I acknowledge mine': its social aspect can be seen in the rival business concern or the figure of the school cad: of its modern incidence the gas ovens of concentration camps bear all too horrible witness.

Perhaps man's greatest shadow has always been what is called death, for it is 'the primordial symbol of the decay and dissolution of the personality'.[12] It is the greatest threat to the conscious position, and one which is bound sooner or later to prevail as long as consciousness is body- and ego-centred.

'What is it all, if we all of us end but in being our own corpse-coffins at last?'[13]

The shadow of death can only become meaningful, and therefore be tolerated, from the standpoint of totality. Any move out of the impasse outlined above involves therefore an appeal to the actuality of that part of human personality which, unlike the physical body and the conscious ego, is in fact deathless as well as shadowless. We shall be seeing that it is that part which Jung in his practice and researches has repeatedly revealed in terms of contemporary intelligibility.

'Strictly speaking, Science does not know of death, but only of change, for science uses the word "death" only to connote a

natural process, an end to every form of life—a part of the
cycle of life, to be observed in all nature. Seed, shoot, bud,
flower, fruit, seed is the complete cycle: why regard any of
these changes as climacteric?'[14]

The answer lies in an understanding of what, according to
Jung and others, occurs at a certain critical point in the form of a
psychosis or more generally and less clinically in any crisis of
human affairs which is acceptably surmounted.

What is involved in this enterprise is splendidly set out in
Lewis Mumford's interpretation of Herman Melville's classic
novel *Moby Dick*.[15] Here is depicted an essential phase in the
search for wholeness, which necessitates the acceptance by man
of his own shadow, which in turn implies a belief in the value of
evil and a meaning to death. In his pursuit of the white whale
Captain Ahab himself becomes the image of the thing he hates:

'By physical defiance, by physical combat, Ahab cannot rout
and capture Moby Dick, the odds are against him, and if his
defiance is noble, his methods are ill chosen. . . . It is easier to
wage war than to conquer in oneself the tendency to be partial,
vindictive and unjust: it is easier to demolish one's enemy than
to pit oneself against him in an intellectual combat which will
disclose one's own weaknesses and provincialities. And that
evil Ahab seeks to strike is the sum of one's enemies. He does
not bow down to it and accept it: therein lie his heroism and
his virtue, but he fights it with his own weapons and therein lies
his madness. All the things that Ahab despises when he is
about to attack the whale, the love and loyalty of Pip, the
memory of his wife and child, the sextant of science, his inner
sense of calm, which makes all external struggle futile, are the
very things that would redeem him and make him victorious.

'Man's ultimate defence against the Universe, against evil
and accident and malice, is not by any fictitious resolution of
these things into an Absolute which justifies them and utilizes
them for its own ends. . . . Man's defence lies within himself,
not within the narrow, isolated ego, which may be overwhelmed,
but in that self which we share with our fellows and which
assures us that, whatever happens to our carcasses and hides,
good men will remain to carry on the work, to foster and pro-
tect the things we have recognized as excellent.'

Now let us follow Jung's explanation of how that self is in fact constellated:

'The religious consciousness is awakened when we encounter a network of contradictions running through our human life. . . . We cannot regain the sense of security until we take hold of something over-riding the contradictions.'[16]

The 'something over-riding the contradictions' Jung has called a 'spiritual inner authority which decides the outcome of conflicting Duties or Tendencies.'

He teaches that the psychological development of the individual consists in his eventually, though perhaps not completely, being able consciously to control that which previously has only been unconscious in him and therefore uncontrollable by him. When this stage is reached, the directional and operational centre, so to speak, of his being shifts from the Ego—the centre of conscious personality—to the Self or centre of total personality. 'Conscious wholeness consists in successful union of Ego and Self so that both preserve their intrinsic qualities.'[17]

The process of attaining conscious wholeness as described by Jung does not necessarily carry any theological implications: he himself constantly insists that he is merely reporting on phenomena he had observed. Nevertheless the self, as thus described, bears unmistakably the same kind of marks and seems to perform the same kind of functions as does what theologians call the Godhead Immanent, the 'Inner Light' of the Quakers, the Atman of the Brahman, the Jewel in the Lotus. Its existence helps to explain the remark of a twentieth-century young man, 'I don't believe in God but I respond to Him.' From quite a different source there is a comparable affirmation in literary terms of the psychological process by means of which archetypal energy can be transformed into conscious spirit:

'For those of us who cannot accept the dogmas of any religion as uniquely revealed by God, faith may be possible that the more universal ideas or patterns underlying these doctrines are God-given, their evolution into greater clarity and relevance to life part of the Divine intention for man.'[18]

An excellent specific example of the application of this idea is to be found in Katherine M. Wilson's study of Keats' *Endymion*.[19]

We may remember Keats' own sage counsel to the effect that men are 'not souls till they acquire identities', till each one is personally himself, until in psychological terms he has become individuated, and then, according to Keats, 'pleasure has no show of enticement and pain no unbearable powers.'

It should be perfectly possible for the non-theist as well as the theist to concentrate on the 'more universal ideas or patterns and the conviction of a purposive evolution' without, unless so inclined by psychological type, attaching a transcendental importance to the words 'God' and 'Divine'.

Along this second avenue of advance our investigation of depth psychology has at least given grounds for renewed belief in the possibility of experiencing wholeness, though the question whether this is to be equated with holiness we leave open; it has also given grounds for belief in the value of evil, and belief in death as an episode, always obliterating body and ego, but not affecting the Self so far as it has been achieved—'death does not touch it at all'. It is not fortuitous that in that phrase ancient Hindu wisdom (see Chapter I) and modern western psychology find their correspondence. Both indicate that life is a phenomenon in process of becoming conscious of itself and that individual human beings are the more or less willing agents whereby that consciousness is being achieved.

Our third avenue of advance is by modern science, and here too, especially through what we are beginning to discover about biology and parapsychology, it is the theme of emerging consciousness which becomes dominant. Two quotations from authoritative sources can best introduce this section:

'In the sciences the tendency to seek a logical or causally homogeneous description of natural things (designed after the pattern of mathematics) is on the decline. It is giving way to a trend originating in philosopy, psychology and atomic physics, to stress the bi-polar character of the phenomenal world and of time. The new trend is changing the structure of the sciences. Foreshadowed in Nicholas of Cusa's *Co-incidentia Oppositorium* and similar conceptions in Eastern and Western philosophers, this description, though logically not homogeneous, is only apparently contradictory: it is bi-polar; that is, it expresses simultaneously two views which, though different, are both requisite to our picture of a particular object. This transformation of science, because of its archetypal character, may lead to a new correspondence between the sciences and the humanities based on a dual (dynamic and dimensional) description of matter.'[20]

Such reflections find an echo in Sir George Thompson's Presidential Address to the British Association in 1960:

'We have been forced, some of us very unwillingly, to believe that at bottom the laws of physics are not statements of what must happen but of the relative chances of a variety of alternatives.'

With such utterances in mind, it is not surprising to find Sir Alister Hardy striding magnificently along our third avenue in his first of two series of Gifford Lectures. The book which contains them is entitled *The Living Stream: A Restatement of Evolution Theory and Its Relation to the Spirit of Man*. In it he makes a case for a Natural Theology which is compatible with, and perhaps even essential to, the comprehension of modern science. He begins by making a distinction:

'Natural Theology has usually maintained that God's existence could be proved as convincingly as a theorem of Euclid, by reason alone—to this I do not subscribe. The Natural Theology I am interested in concerns a Theism which is derived empirically from the study of nature, man and human history.'[21]

He proceeds to distinguish his own position even from that of Sir Julian Huxley, who probably because of his association with Pierre Teilhard de Chardin, is regarded, wrongly, according to Sir Alister, as holding a religious viewpoint. In order to dissociate himself from it, he quotes the following passage from Huxley's *Religion without Revelation*, which is of particular interest to us in the context of our previous discussion of the Soul and the 'Godhead Immanent'.

'. . . This question of God or no-God, external power or no external power, non-human absolute values against human evolving values, this question is fundamental. Until it is settled and the idea of God relegated to the past with the idea of ritual magic and other products of primitive and unscientific human thought, we shall never get the new religion we need. . . . Once we have rid ourselves of this doctrine of Divine Power external to ourselves, we can get busy with the real task of dealing with our inner forces.

'This', says Sir Alister, 'is where I feel a discussion of evolution theory in relation to natural theology is so important. Has modern biology destroyed the basis for a theistic religion? I should at once explain that by theism I do not mean a belief in a deity with an anthropomorphic image. I do, however, at least mean—and this is where I differ from Huxley—a belief in an "extra-sensory" contact with a Divine Power which is greater than and in part lies beyond the individual self: towards this we have a feeling, no doubt for good biological or psychological reasons (linked with the emotions of an early child-parent affection, but none the worse for that) of a personal relationship, and we can call it God.'[22]

At this point, and before following Sir Alister's argument about Natural Theology further, it is useful to recall Tyrrell's distinction in the previous chapter between spiritualism and psychical research, and to emphasize the fact that we are here concerned with the latter.

William James once remarked in a letter to his brother Henry:

'The richest field for new discoveries is the odd, unclassified residuum. Round the brim of each of those neat and orderly systems we call science there lurks a handful of queer and unaccountable phenomena, often trifling in themselves, which when brought into the open and scrutinized more closely, have furnished the starting points of entirely new conceptions. The most striking instances are those out-of-the-way anomalies which, when systematically re-investigated during the early years of the present century, gave rise to the quantum theory, and so revolutionized the whole basis of modern science. There are similar unexplained peculiarities in the field of human behaviour. The strange occurrences reported from time to time which suggest the notions of such dramatic processes as telepathy, clairvoyance and pre-cognition form the most baffling elements in the unclassified residuum left on one side in the academic study of the mind.'[23]

'Telepathy is something which ought not to happen at all, if the Materialist Theory were true. But it does happen. So there must be something seriously wrong with the Materialistic Theory however numerous and imposing the normal facts which support it may be. . . . If they (the queer facts of psychical research) show, as I think they do, that the Materialistic conception of human personality is untenable, and if they throw a new light on the age-old conflict between the scientific and the religious outlooks, we shall have to conclude that Psychical Research is one of the most important branches of investigation which the human mind has ever undertaken.'[24]

Instead of pursuing further here the implications of this revolutionary theory, three references must suffice:

(a) Geraldine Cummins, *Swan on a Black Sea*, Routledge, 1965.*
(b) Michel Bouissou, *Life of a Sensitive*, Sidgwick and Jackson, 1955.
(c) Raynor C. Johnson, *The Imprisoned Splendour*, Hodder and Stoughton, 1953.*

On p. 253 of *The Living Stream*, Sir Alister Hardy writes:

'I must now come to the point of saying just why I believe the recognition of the reality of telepathy may be so important for biology. If it is proved to exist in man, and I believe the evidence is overwhelming, and if we believe that man is one with the stream of life, then it seems that it is most unlikely that so remarkable a phenomenon should be confined to just a few individuals or just one species of animal. If true, this faculty whereby one individual influences another by means other than through the ordinary senses is surely one of the most revolutionary discoveries of natural history.

'. . . My "vitalism" is a belief that there is a psychic side of the animal which, apart from inherited instinctive behaviour, may be independent of the D.N.A., the code that governs the form of the physical frame but that it may inter-act with the physical system in the evolutionary process through organic selection.'

Denying ourselves the pleasure of pursuing further Sir Alister's speculations on the significance of this connection between biology and telepathy, let us once again take up his thoughts on Natural Theology.

'Whilst Science cannot bring religions into being I do believe that the spirit of scientific inquiry can help in the re-establishment of "a declining faith" . . . I believe that only a theology based upon a scientific approach as advocated by Lord Gifford can survive in the intellectual atmosphere of the future.'

The suggestion is then made that it is through a deeper understanding especially in the biological treatment of the nature of consciousness that such a theory can be constructed. On p. 275 he quotes from Sir Ronald Fisher's Eddington Memorial Lecture on 'Creative Aspects of Natural Law' the following passages:

'The surface or limit separating the inner from the outer life of each living thing is also, in our experience, the true seat of our consciousness, the boundary of the objective and the subjective, where we experience, through our imperfect sense-organs, what comes to us from outside and, with at least equal obscurity, that which rises into consciousness from within. If consciousness is, as it would seem, the symbol, or even the means, of unification in each being, this is the region to which creative activity could most fitly be traced.

'It is in this field (that of experiments in telepathy)', continues Sir Alister, 'that I believe science will come to make its second great contribution to natural theology by showing the reality of part of the Universe outside the world of the physical senses. It is in this apparently non-material part of the world that the power we call God must lie: some source of influences to which Man can have access in an extra-sensory way by the communicative act we call prayer.'[25]

'I believe that the living world is as closely linked with theology as it is with physics and chemistry: that the Divine element is part of the natural process—not strictly supernatural but para-physical.'[26]

'At the very least, I expect this power of which we speak may be some sub-conscious shared reservoir of spiritual "know-how" which we call Divine (perhaps something like the "species mind") that I have suggested; I think, however, it is far more likely that above this there is something much more wonderful to which we give the name God. But even if it should be shown, and I do not believe it will, that this whole conception is a purely psychological one and, if, in some way, this mind factor should eventually be proved to be entirely of physico-chemical origin—it would not to my mind destroy the joy or help of the experience we may still call Divine any more than it would destroy the glorious beauty felt in poetry or art.'

Our third avenue of advance has at least revealed a forthright declaration of belief by an eminent scientist in the company of his peers.

One hundred years ago there appeared the following reflection in Hawthorne's *Journal on Melville* (1856):

'He can neither believe, nor be comfortable in his unbelief, and he is too honest and courageous not to try to be one or the other.'

Various attempts, as we have seen in the previous chapters, have been made to believe and not to believe. We have studied the effects of this endeavour on the traditional religious creeds and on their secular alternatives; we have examined our present prospects in the mirrors of art, depth psychology and modern science.[27] Perhaps the fairest assessment that can yet be made is something like this: the twentieth century has witnessed the discovery of a new dimension of consciousness; in its appeal to our understanding lies our hope, if not our belief.

REFERENCES

1. *Selected Papers on Philosophy*, p. 124.
2. HELLER, ERICH: *The Ironic German.*
3. p. 127.
4. PLOWMAN, MAX: *The Right to Live* (Andrew Dakers, 1942).*
5. READ, HERBERT: *Icon and Idea* (Faber and Faber, 1955), pp. 91–3.*
6. op. cit., p. 101.
7. HEARD, G.: *Pain, Sex and Time* (Cassell, 1939).*
8. WEIL, SIMONE: *Notebooks*, Vol. 2, p. 414 (Routledge, 1956).
9. Phrase of Lucien Lévy-Bruhl in *La Mentalité Primitive* (Allen and Unwin, 1928).
10. Quoted from a report on one of Jung's seminars.
11. See CATHER, WILLA: *My Mortal Enemy* (Hamish Hamilton, 1963).*
12. NEUMANN, ERICH: *Origins and Growth of Consciousness* (Routledge, 1954), p. 221.*

13. TENNYSON, ALFRED, LORD: 'Vastness'.
14. PLOWMAN, MAX: *The Right to Live* (Andrew Dakers, 1942)*—from an essay entitled 'What does Death mean to me?'
15. See MUMFORD, L.: *The Human Prospect* (Secker and Warburg, 1956),* pp. 40–1.
16. SUZUKI, D. T.: *Mysticism, Christian and Buddhist* (Allen and Unwin, 1957),* p. 147.
17. See, for elaboration of this thought, JUNG, C. G.: *The Structure and Dynamics of the Psyche: Collected Works* (Routledge, 1957), Vol. 8, and Chapter 4 of Vol. 9, Part 2.
18. BODKIN, MAUD: *Studies of Type—Images in Poetry, Religion and Philosophy* (O.U.P., 1951).*
19. WILSON, KATHERINE M.: *The Nightingale and The Hawk; a Psychological Study of Keats' Ode* (Allen & Unwin, 1965).*
20. KNOLL, MAX: 'Transformations of Science in Our Age' from *Eranos Yearbooks*. No. 3, *Man and Time* (Routledge & Kegan Paul, 1956).*
21. HARDY, Sir ALISTER: *The Living Stream* (Collins, 1965), p. 11.*
22. op. cit., p. 21.
23. BURT, Sir CYRIL: from the introduction of HEYWOOD, ROSALIND: *The Infinite Hive: a Personal Record of Extra-Sensory Experience.*
24. PRICE, Prof. H. H.: *Hibbert Journal* (Allen & Unwin, 1949), Vol. 47, pp. 105–13.
25. HARDY, Sir A.: op. cit., p. 282.
26. op. cit., p. 284.
27. See THORPE, W. H.: *Science, Man and Morals* (Methuen, 1965), especially p. xi: '. . . The impressive and growing understanding of the unitary foundation underlying all experience, scientific, artistic and religious.'*